Endorsements

"As we scan the headlines that scream of youth turned bad, we shake our heads and wonder what went wrong. Committing to a child has all but gone out of style today, and America's children are suffering for it. Bonnie Fite deserves five stars as her reward for reminding us that child discipline is crucial to society! This book is an excellent resource . . . . "

Beverly LaHaye
Chairman, Concerned Women for America

"Bonnie Fite is a godly lady who thinks and writes biblically. Her excellent work on *Effective Discipline - A Delicate Balance* reflects her commitment to principles of discipline and training based on God's Word. In baseball terms, 'she covers all the bases,' and has offered to her readers a full range of discipline situations and remedies that are practical for teachers and parents."

Paul A. Kienel
Founder and President Emeritus
Association of Christian Schools International

"*Effective Discipline* is a timely book based on timely principles . . . a book that will enhance every parent's and teacher's library . . . easy to read, well organized, and detailed enough to help in any perplexing discipline dilemma. I heartily recommend *Effective Discipline* to every parent and teacher."

William L. Lien
Principal, Assistant Principal, Curriculum Advisor, and teacher for 40 years

"What impressed me most was how biblical and practical her steps were, and how peaceful I felt in using them with my children."

Linda Wong
Teacher and parent.

"As a pediatric nurse, I see so many families with discipline problems . . . Often parents have no one to turn to for advice. I believe that this book will be a vital tool for all these people."

Bianca C. Frederick, RN
Pediatric Charge Nurse.

Effective Discipline

A Delicate Balance

For further information contact:

Bonnie J. Fite
Effective Discipline Seminars
P.O. Box 70434
Sunnyvale, California 94086
(408) 245-7245

Effective Discipline

A Delicate Balance

Bonnie Johnson Fite

Effective Discipline - A Delicate Balance
by Bonnie Johnson Fite
ISBN 0-88270-738-8
Library of Congress Catalog Card Number: Pending
Copyright © 1997 by Bonnie Johnson Fite

Published by:
BRIDGE-LOGOS *Publishers*
North Brunswick Corporate Center
1300 Airport Road, Suite E
North Brunswick, NJ 08902-1700

Dedication

To John, my life's partner and
best friend.
Without your patience,
encouragement, and support
throughout the long process of
birthing this book, it never would
have been delivered.

Contents

There are two pains in life: the pain of discipline, or the pain of regret.

Author unknown

Preface

If we put 100 Christian parents and teachers in a room and asked them to give us their advice on child discipline, they would give us 100 different answers. If we sorted and categorized them, they would probably fall into three distinct camps.

The first camp would focus on correction. Bible verses that use the rod would become their foundation. Outsiders might call them negative or harsh. They are unconcerned about what others might say because they use Scripture as their base.

The second camp reacts to the first group by swinging the pendulum in the opposite direction. The bumper sticker "Question Authority" could be their motto. They feel that children have rights—rights to select their own rules and punishments, and they should be an equal to their parents and teachers. The home or classroom becomes a democracy. The parents no longer parent, they merely guide. The teacher no longer teaches, she facilitates. These "enlightened" adults have little distinguishing them from the popular secular leaders of today.

The third camp also uses Scripture as their base. The heavenly Father becomes their role model. The verses on the rod are only one part of their overall approach to discipline. Parents and teachers recognize the biblical chain of command and the importance of their authority. This is not a democracy, nor is it a harsh dictatorship. Benevolent, loving, leadership distinguishes this camp. Children are seen as a sheep in need of a shepherd. As the children grow and become more responsible, they receive more freedom. One day, when they're grown, they'll have all the rights and privileges of adults, but that won't happen until they are adults.

If you find yourself in either of the first two camps and feel frustrated as you discipline the children in your care, let me show you a plan of biblical balance.

Bonnie Fite
Sunnyvale, CA
1996

1

Is There Hope?

She was hopeless. She shrank back from the warm spring sunshine. Dirt and tears streaked down her face, while her light brown hair hung tangled. Her outfit was filthy. This was one of many bad days when she refused to let anyone wash her face or comb her hair.

Snarling like a wild animal, she lunged at anyone who dared come near her. Recently, in a fit of rage, she nearly injured her baby sister by dumping her out of the cradle.

Her parents were not poor, they were wealthy, prominent members of their community. They loved her deeply and often looked at her with sorrowful, sympathetic eyes.

She spoke only with grunts and snarls. At six years of age, she was growing larger, stronger, and more dangerous each day. Her desperate parents knew if something didn't change soon, she would need to live in an institution. In a last attempt, they hired a specialist to come and work with their daughter.

On March 5, the "specialist" arrived. They didn't know she was straight out of school and had no teaching

1

experience. She didn't know that she had just stepped into a live war zone.

The girl hurled herself like a ferocious dog at her new teacher. One day, she knocked out her teacher's two front teeth.

In spite of all the abuse she received, the teacher saw potential in her young student. She saw glimpses of intelligence underneath the storm of anger. At first she tried to win the girl over with gentleness and affection. Within a few days she realized this was not enough. She needed to balance the love and affection with clear boundaries and firmness.

Her first goal was to help her little student act like a civilized human and not like an animal. Whenever the girl didn't get her way, she would fly into vicious tantrums. These tantrums had been very effective for her in the past, but now they were fruitless. Her anger grew as the teacher expected more civil behavior from her.

Finally one morning at breakfast, a full-blown war broke out. Her parents had never expected her to sit at the table and eat with the rest of them. Instead she roamed around the table foraging for food from any nearby plates. Since this was common practice, everyone kept on talking and eating as if nothing was wrong. The teacher could take it no longer. When the girl reached onto her plate, the teacher pushed her hands away. The startled girl tried again. This time her hand was slapped. The girl recoiled in anger. The teacher got up, held her by the shoulders and firmly planted her on a chair. Then she put a spoon in her hand and began scooping up food. The girl hurled her spoon to the floor. Undaunted, the teacher made her get out of the chair and pick up the spoon. At this point, the parents left the room in disgust. The teacher again planted her student on a chair and helped her scoop up food on a spoon. Again the girl threw her spoon on the floor. Then she jumped on top of it, refusing to move.

The teacher sat down and continued to eat her breakfast. The girl snuck up behind her and tried to pull the teacher's chair out from under her. When the girl failed at this, she started to pinch her teacher. Then the teacher pushed the girl away, got up and planted her in a chair again. She placed the spoon in her small hand, and scooped up more food. Finally hunger won out and the girl reluctantly ate.

A few hours later, a subdued girl finished her meal, and went out to play, while her exhausted teacher retired to her room and wept. Little did she know that this small, yet costly victory was the start of a major breakthrough.

In the exhausting weeks that followed, she doggedly worked with the girl, determined to break through and bring order to her chaotic world. Gradually the girl acted more civilized. Her fits of rage subsided as she developed more self-control and learned to express herself appropriately. One month later on April 5, 1887, the breakthrough occurred. The teacher, Annie Sullivan, taught her student to spell the word *water*, using the manual alphabet. Who was her wild little student? *Helen Keller.* The rest is history.

A novice teacher wisely implemented timeless principles of effective discipline. She broke into a forlorn, neglected little girl's dark world and pulled her out. She loved her even when she was unlovely. Her greatest strengths were her hope—hope in a better life for Helen and her determination to make that hope become reality.

Annie Sullivan's words to Captain and Mrs. Keller echo back over the century to parents and teachers today. "Don't feel sorry for her anymore. She's not a poor little thing, she's brighter than most children. And I'm going to help her be as normal as possible."

Whether children in your care have minor to severe behavior problems, the timeless principles of effective discipline offer solutions. These principles originate in Scripture and are woven throughout this writing. The goal of this book is to give parents and teachers hope. A practical system of discipline that has been successful in the home and the classroom will show parents and teachers how to establish discipline. Then it will be up to you, the reader, to provide the determination to make your hope become reality.

First it's important to define some terms.

2
Definitions

Olivia looks on from the wings as the flurry of ballet dancers exit. The music halts. As silence fills the Toronto theater, Olivia floats across the stage. Every eye is riveted to her solitary form. Each controlled muscle obeys her command. Power pours out of every limb as she gracefully personifies peace. For a magical moment, the audience feels this peace.

Olivia has given many years of her life for this moment of perfection. At the age of thirteen she left home to study ballet. While other teens were dating and cheering at basketball games, she was practicing, practicing, practicing. On top of her schooling and studies, she spent over 25 hours a week training each muscle to obey with precision. Since there is no dialogue in ballet, a dancer must speak through her slightest movement. *This is the epitome of discipline.*

Let's look closer at some terms to grasp a fuller understanding of discipline.

External and Internal Discipline

The first term we need to look at is *discipline*. The dictionary defines it four different ways: (1) training that corrects or molds moral character, (2) teaching orderly conduct, (3) teaching control, and (4) self-control. This definition encompasses two different types of discipline.

The first three definitions (with the words training, molding, and teaching) describe external discipline. This type of discipline is imposed from outside the child by a teacher or parent. For instance, most children don't want to practice the same songs over and over again. If they are to excel at piano playing, they will need an adult who forces them to practice on a daily basis. Most children can learn a new skill much faster than adults, but they need to have external discipline applied to them if they are to acquire these new skills.

The last part of the dictionary's definition is "self-control." This is the second type of discipline. This internal discipline comes from within the child. There are a few children who seem to have been born with this self-control—they are the ones who become Olympic athletes and famous musicians. Olivia, the ballerina, is a good example of this type of child. She had the internal discipline necessary to become a world-class dancer. Most children don't have such strong internal discipline early in life and need help from parents and teachers to develop it.

The goal of a parent or teacher is to apply external discipline (the training that corrects or molds moral character, and the teaching of orderly conduct and control) to enable a child to develop new skills and proper conduct. Once this is achieved, the parent or teacher should gradually phase out the external discipline as the internal discipline (self-control) takes root in the child.

When I was toilet training my son, he received a

6

treat every time he successfully used the toilet, but I knew that by the time he entered school, no one would praise him and give him a treat for successful toilet use. Once he mastered his new skill, we gradually phased out his treats. When we first started training him, he would receive one treat (a mini-marshmallow or gummi bear) just for sitting on the potty and trying. When he successfully "went," he got two treats. Once he began going consistently, we stopped any rewards for merely trying.

Later, when he was mostly trained, we would give him an extra treat for going when he needed to go without us reminding him. Soon, he only got treats for successfully going without any reminders. Once he mastered this, we began giving him treats for successfully staying dry through the night. Instead of highlighting the reward he would no longer receive (i.e., for trying to go) we strongly emphasized the new reward. At all times these rewards were accompanied with a lot of praise. We would say things like, "We're so proud of you. Now you know when it's time for you to go to the potty. You're a very big boy!"

This is similar to the parent who puts training wheels on a child's bike. These extra wheels provide additional support as the child learns to balance. As the child's balance improves, the wheels are gradually lifted until one day they're no longer necessary. The child has developed his or her own internal sense of balance.

This principle also works in the classroom. Each year, I started out by teaching the students our classroom routine. I used lots of external discipline, like frequent rewards and punishments, until the students adjusted to our routine. Then I gradually phased out this emphasis on our basic routine and focused on higher levels of behavior. Once we had adjusted to the basic routine, I was free to look for kids who were being courteous, or helpful to their neighbor. When I saw selfless acts such as these, I rewarded these children and gave them lots of recognition.

Reward

Another term we need to understand is *reward*. The dictionary defines this as "something given in return for good or worthy behavior." I've often heard people use the term "bribe" when they reward their children, but they are missing an important distinction. That same dictionary defines bribe as "to give money or favors to induce someone to act dishonestly, to seduce." Given these definitions, you should see a big distinction between rewards and bribes. It's all in the motive of the person who is giving the reward.

Do we want a child to do what is right or what is wrong? As long as we reward a child for doing what is right and noble, then no one can accuse us of bribery. If someone does accuse you of bribery, don't feel guilty. Once again, you're following God's example. James 1:13 reads, "When tempted, no one should say, 'God is tempting me.' For God cannot be tempted by evil, nor does he tempt anyone." God doesn't tempt anyone, but freely bestows blessings or rewards on His people. This is only one of numerous examples of God rewarding His people for doing right. Another example is shown in Daniel 1:8-20.

Daniel was a young man of principle who "resolved not to defile himself with the royal food and wine, and he asked the chief official for permission not to defile himself this way" (Daniel 1:8). Because he chose to obey God's laws, God blessed him by giving him favor in the eyes of the commander and knowledge and understanding of all kinds of literature and learning. Daniel could understand visions and dreams of all kinds (Daniel 1:17). In every matter on which the king questioned him, he found him ten times better than all the magicians and enchanters in his whole kingdom (Daniel 1:20). Daniel was placed in the personal service of the king along with his three friends, most commonly known as Shadrach, Meshach, and Abednego. Because they were faithful to God and remained obedient, they were blessed with position and prestige.

Rewards and incentives are a natural part of life, and do not cease as children grow into adults. Employers give bonuses to devoted employees. The IRS rewards contributions to charitable organizations by allowing the taxable income to be deducted. Even car-pool lanes were developed to reward people who commute together.

Punishment

The next term we should understand is *punishment*. The dictionary defines this as "to impose a penalty for an offense." Just as the Bible shows God rewarding His people, Scripture is also filled with examples of God punishing His people. In Judges 13:19-21, Samson immediately received his punishment for having a shaved head—he lost his superhuman strength.

In the creation story, Adam and Eve were punished by God for eating the forbidden fruit. They were driven from the Garden of Eden and given a life of toil. But the ultimate punishment for their disobedience was their spiritual death—that is, separation from God.

God consistently uses rewards and punishment whether He works with individuals or groups. God deals with the entire nation of Israel in Deuteronomy 7:9-15. He tells them that He is a faithful God, keeping His covenant with those who love Him and keep His commandments. If they follow His commands, He will heap blessings on them by providing abundant crops, increasing their livestock, multiplying their offspring, and protecting them from sickness and disease. Later, in Deuteronomy 8:19-20, God warns them that forgetting Him and His commands and following other gods will lead to their destruction.

God created this world with a natural law of cause and effect. This natural law makes consequences—rewards and punishment—a result of right or wrong actions.

There was one time when God intervened with this natural law of cause and effect. It happened when Jesus died and took the consequences of our sins upon Himself. Eternal life in heaven is the one reward we can never earn. It is a free gift from God, as expressed in Ephesians 2:8-9: "For it is by grace you have been saved, through faith—and this is not from yourselves, it is the gift of God—not by works, so that no one can boast."

Effective Discipline

Finally, here is my own definition of discipline. The word *discipline* often brings negative connotations to mind, but it has a very positive application. I see discipline as "training in conduct that uses a neutral blend of rewards and punishment to shape moral character." The term *neutral blend of rewards and punishment* is used to stress the importance of balancing the necessary punishment with lots of love, warmth, and affection whenever the child does right. This blend will help to produce a child with solid moral character.

Effective discipline is a delicate balance between affirmation and punishment. If a parent or teacher neglects one or both of these aspects on a regular basis, the child will suffer. The chart below shows the four ways children can be affected by their parents' right or wrong use of affirmation and punishment.

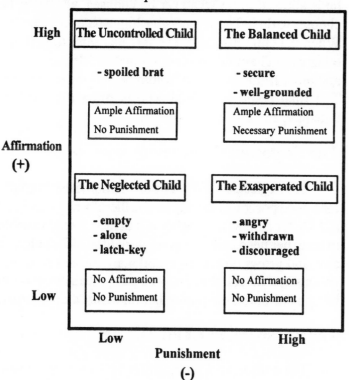

The term *affirmation*, as used in this chart, encompasses all the positive things a parent or teacher does to encourage the child. This includes rewards, praise, love, and affection. Rewards are directly linked to a child's good behavior. However, affection and encouragement—words like, "I'm so glad you're my child"—should be given out generously regardless of a child's behavior. A child who is being punished must be reassured of his parent's or teacher's love.

The Uncontrolled Child

The uncontrolled child grows up in a home where he is allowed to do whatever he chooses, whenever he chooses to do it. The parents give him whatever he wants. When the child disobeys, the parents prefer to look the other way. The child becomes spoiled and demands more and more from his parents whom he no longer respects. The final result is a child who is often dissatisfied, unhappy, and disliked by others.

The Neglected Child

The neglected child grows up in a home that is empty for a good portion of the day, and is therefore a "latchkey" kid. Or her parents may be home, but they are unavailable to meet her needs. She receives very little affirmation, if any, and grows up feeling emotionally distant from her parents and others. Since no one pays much attention to her, no one bothers to punish her for disobedience either.

The Exasperated Child

The exasperated child grows up in a home where he receives very little, if any, affirmation. Unfortunately, his parents are suspicious of him and watch closely for any infractions of the family rules. When he does disobey, he is punished severely. As a result, the child becomes angry, withdrawn, and discouraged, feeling trapped in a no-win situation with his parents. These children often grow up feeling they are bad people and carry a lot of false guilt.

Both the neglected and the exasperated child concern me the most. They grow up deprived of affirmation and affection, which are basic emotional needs of every human being. As Dr. James Dobson of *Focus on the Family* once said in a radio broadcast, "They are like fragile plants struggling to grow without water." Any "neglected" or "exasperated" student that ended up in my classroom received extra affirmation and affection from me in an effort to help meet this very basic need.

The Well-Balanced Child

The well-balanced child has had the privilege of growing up in a home where she receives ample affirmation and affection. When she disobeys, she receives the necessary and appropriate punishment. This gives her security and confidence. Her parents have found the delicate balance between rewards and punishment.

One last word on balance. A little punishment can go a long way, while affirmation should be given out liberally. A child should always receive more affirmation than punishment.

How will these definitions of discipline, reward, bribe, punishment, and the need for balance impact the role of a teacher or parent?

13

Style of Discipline

It's also important for both parents to agree on the style of discipline that should be used. But keep in mind that when a difference of opinion arises, the parents should discuss it privately. Children should not see disagreements between the parents, especially when the parents are dealing with them.

It's very confusing for a child to grow up in a home where each parent is using a different form of discipline. Most common is the family where the father is harsh and may even be abusive. The mother, in an effort to compensate, becomes indulgent and doting. Even if one parent refuses to be rational in their disciplining, however, the other parent must try to present a balanced approach to discipline. It's better to have at least one parent giving the child a balanced environment, than neither parent.

Abusive Home

If the father is genuinely abusive to the mother or the child, then the mother must seek outside help from a counselor or pastor. She and the child should not be forced to remain in an abusive setting. At the two Christian schools where I taught, most children came from stable family environments. But one family from each school struggled with serious abuse at home. In both families this escalated to the point where one parent shot and killed the other parent. For that reason, much of this book deals with prevention. If you're involved in an abusive home, get help while the situation is small, before it escalates. This will also help prevent the pattern of abuse from repeating itself in the next generation.

Help for Teachers

Whether in a school or a church setting, teachers have the authority over their students. As long as the child is in the teacher's care, the teacher is responsible for providing a balanced, orderly environment so the children can learn. The next three chapters will help teachers establish a balanced, orderly classroom environment, filled with warmth and excitement.

Help for Parents

Many modern parents are convinced that only the experts know how to train children. They focus on building a successful career and leave the training to the experts. Often these parents prefer the peace and quiet of the office to the chaos at home. This shouldn't be. These successful career people can also be successful parents. If you are among these parents, with this book you can become experts about your own children.

Whether you're a mother who stays home full-time, or who works outside the home and earns a paycheck, or a combination of these two, this book will give you the tools you need to establish a more peaceful, balanced, loving home environment.

A single mother has an especially difficult task. When she's exhausted at the end of a hectic day, she doesn't have a husband who will come home and share the burden of disciplining the children. She bears all the parental authority in her home. She especially needs to pray frequently, asking God for His wisdom, strength, and courage. Even more so, this book will give the single parent the tools to bring order and peace into the home.

Applying the principles in this book will buy back precious time and effort in later years.

Balanced Discipline

As you the parent or teacher implement the following discipline system, it will help you achieve the delicate balance of effective discipline. It will take time and consistency to establish it, but once you and the child or children have adjusted to it, you will all benefit from having more quality time to enjoy each other and less time spent in warfare. In short, the amount of time spent implementing this system will be paid back with big dividends later on.

In summary, God, our heavenly Father is an excellent role model. Throughout the Scriptures He establishes a pattern of using rewards and punishments to lead mankind back to Him.

3
Basic Principles

As you establish your own discipline system, shaped to fit your specific situation, keep in mind the following four basic principles:

1. Maximize the trainable years.
2. With responsibility comes privilege.
3. The punishment should match the offense.
4. Consistency and follow-through are essential.

Maximize the Trainable Years

Proverbs 22:6 says, "Train up a child in the way he should go, and when he is old, he will not depart from it" (NKJV). Children are so impressionable in the early years. They are like wet clay that can easily be shaped, but as time moves on they become harder and more set in their ways. Up to 85% of a child's personality is formed in the first five years of life.

As this next story illustrates, a mother can make a profound lifelong impression on her young children. Luis Palau, a famous evangelist, once told the story of a Russian dignitary and the KGB officer who was assigned to stay with him and prevent him from defecting. While both were attending a dinner party with evangelical leaders in the Netherlands, they sat as far apart from each other as possible. Each of them confided in their table partner that from the time he was young, he learned about God at his mother's knee and each man had a deeply rooted faith in God. In order to progress in his career, either as a diplomat or with the KGB, each man kept his deeply held beliefs private and went through all the motions of a good Communist. What those two mothers instilled in their young boys withstood all the years of Soviet brainwashing.

Deuteronomy 6:5-7 says, "Love the LORD your God with all your heart and with all your soul and with all your strength. These commandments that I give you today are to be upon your hearts. Impress them on your children. Talk about them when you sit at home and when you walk along the road, when you lie down and when you get up."

Although this commandment was intended for parents, it can also be applied to teachers who are often the "caregivers" of the children for the better part of the day. Parents and teachers should constantly look for opportunities to tell children about God. Teaching a child about God and His truth should be woven into the fabric of daily living at home and at school.

Whenever a toy is lost in our home, I have my son pray and ask Jesus to help him find the lost toy. To start, I pray and my son repeats my prayer. Eventually, each of my sons will learn to pray on his own, "Dear Jesus, please help me find my lost bear. Thank you." My oldest son often exclaimed to me, "Mom, Jesus said, 'Yes!'" Well, of course, Jesus never lets him down.

One day we were in the grocery store and I couldn't find the last item on my list. I finally gave up on my search and got ready to pay for the rest of my groceries. My son, John, however, wouldn't let me give up so easily. "But, Mom, we need to pray and ask Jesus to help us." At this point I was in a bad mood and wanted to leave, but despite what the other shoppers might have been thinking, I allowed him to pray. As usual, his little prayer brought results. When at last we pulled up to the checkout counter, I was relieved that I hadn't stood in the way of his growing faith. Someday, he and Jesus may move mountains.

As a teacher, your power of influence over the students in your care will be greatest when they're young. Children from kindergarten through third grade are the most trainable since they usually have an "awe" of teachers. The mother of one of my third graders once asked her son what he thought of me. He responded, "Well, I think of her the same way I think of the President." Now *he* was a trainable boy! Once children reach the age of nine or more, they become more dependent on their peers and don't care as much what teachers and parents think. So, make the most of the time when the children in your care are small.

A word of caution for parents and those who teach young children—God recognizes the great impact we have on these small lives. James 3:1 says, "Not many of you should presume to be teachers, my brothers, because you know that we who teach will be judged more strictly." Make sure that your authority is used to build these little ones into men and women of moral character.

With Responsibility Comes Privilege

The opposite of this basic principle is also true—with irresponsibility comes loss of privilege. It's crucial to make sure that responsibility and privilege are closely linked. I rarely hand out privileges without responsibility being a prerequisite. The more a child connects privileges with responsibility, the more responsible that child will become. Otherwise, a child may grow up expecting privileges and behaving irresponsibly.

When I take my preschool aged children to the grocery store, they have the privilege of driving miniature shopping carts through the store. As long as they don't capsize their little load of groceries, or drive recklessly, and stay close to me, they have the privilege of driving their carts up to the checkout counter and unloading all their groceries like grownups.

This principle also works well in the classroom. I rarely wasted a privilege, such as leading the line or passing out papers, and constantly looked for responsible students to honor.

I also removed privileges from an entire group of students. When my third-grade class became disruptive and noisy, I told them, "Since you're acting like kindergartners, I'm going to take away your third-grade privileges and treat you like kindergartners. You need to put your heads down on your desks." Being treated like a kindergartner was humiliating, so it usually solved the problem quickly. One day I was speaking to a sixth-grade teacher about this. She said whenever her class was acting irresponsibly, she would tell them they were all acting like third-graders!

One privilege that would be a natural result of responsible behavior might be allowing a child to make his own choices. With a young child it should start out small, like selecting which socks to wear with a given outfit. Then as she becomes more responsible, she might select an outfit from two or three options. As time goes on, she gradually earns the right to wear what she chooses as long as it is clean and modest.

This gradual transition of placing more and more responsibility on a child who demonstrates that she is ready for more, can be done with choices in many other areas. Always make sure that additional privileges are linked to responsible behavior. The more responsible child should have more privileges and thus more freedom and choices than an irresponsible child.

Hopefully a child will pick up on this and start moving toward responsibility. Even a teen who gets good grades might have the privilege of taking the car on Friday night—while the same teen who gets bad grades could lose the privilege of going out altogether.

Punishment Should Match the Offense

It's wise never to punish a child too harshly for a minor offense or too lightly for a major offense. Perhaps this basic principle will be most clearly understood by showing an example of a punishment that did not match the offense.

A sixth-grade boy had hair that barely touched the top of his ears. This violated the school dress code at his Christian school, so he was sent home to have it cut. He had it cut 1/16 of an inch above his ear and in no time it touched his ears again. A school board member saw his hair, sent him home, and said if it happened again the boy would be expelled. The school board member told the boy's teacher he had never seen such rebellion in a child. This upset her. She said, of all the boys in her class, he had the best attitude and was basically a good kid. Many of the boys had short enough hair, but were stubborn and unteachable. This threatened punishment clearly did not match the offense.

Chapter eight deals with *rebellion*, which is an arrogant, disrespectful attitude. But this boy was respectful and obedient to his teacher. His hair had been cut to regulation, but it grew longer and touched his ears again. He should not have let it touch his ears, but the fact that it grew longer was not an act of rebellion. He had no control over the speed at which his hair was growing. This minor offense did need to be dealt with, but not so severely. The focus on outward appearance missed the more important issue of internal character.

The board member would have been more effective if he had told the boy, "Well, I'm not very good at haircuts and since this is your second offense, I'll let you go home and have it cut. But the next time you come to school with hair that touches your ears, I'll get out my scissors and make sure that your hair won't hit violation for a long time." Then the board member should have sent a note home to the parents explaining what the boy could expect in the future. If the boy had any sense at all, I'm sure he would make sure he never received an "official" school haircut.

One day my children and I met friends for lunch at a pizza parlor. I forgot to bring my preschooler's bib. Since he was a messy eater, I knew he would end up wearing pizza on his new shirt if I didn't act quickly.

When the pizza arrived, I tucked a paper napkin into his collar. But he pulled out the napkin and refused to wear it. I told him that we had plenty of pizza but I would not let him have a bite until he wore the napkin. I moved the pizza out of arms reach and the rest of us began to eat. He sat in his high chair and fussed for about five minutes. Then he got quiet and said he was ready to wear the napkin. As he devoured his pizza, we were both happy. I knew we had been spared a major battle over this minor issue. As long as he's a messy eater, he'll wear a bib or napkin when he eats.

Consistency and Immediate Follow-through are Essential

This last principle is illustrated in Proverbs 28:23: "He who rebukes a man will find more favor afterward than he who flatters with the tongue." It takes courage to be consistent and follow through with punishment. I put this principle to the test on my first day of student teaching when I was left alone with 27 second graders.

I had just finished telling them to raise their hands if they needed to talk, when Diane spoke out. I reminded her of our rule. Two minutes later, she spoke out again. At this point I struggled with myself as I considered how to deal with Diane. Part of me said, "Aw, give her a break. After all, it's the first day of school and you want Diane to like you. In fact, you want all the kids to think you are nice." On the other hand, I thought, "Remember in your education classes how you were told that you must always follow through with consistent discipline, or the students will lose respect for you. You must keep your word." Luckily,

I listened to the latter voice and firmly took five minutes off Diane's recess. Not only did I gain Diane's respect, but 26 other children were watching. Because they knew I followed through on my word, it prevented many others from speaking out.

This principle also works in the home. When parents threaten to punish their children, but don't follow through on a regular basis, they will find their words have less and less impact. In fact, children can develop a "selective hearing problem," and only hear those things they choose to hear. Make sure your child respects your words and knows they're backed up with firm action.

Children playing at the park may be having such a great time that they don't want to leave when mother says it's time to go home. She may say, "All right now kids, if you don't come right away I'm going to leave without you!" She will take three or four firm steps toward the car. She may even disappear around the corner of a building, but her attempts to scare her children won't work. She's never left them and driven off before, so why should they believe her this time. They know empty threats when they hear them. If this continues, her children will listen to less and less of what she has to say.

It's far more effective for a mother to say, "Kids, you have five more minutes to play and then we need to go." They've been warned that they need to begin winding down their fun. When the time is up, they're told it's time to go. If a child chooses not to come, the mother may give her a choice—she can walk out of the park like a respectable "big kid," or she can be carried out like a little kid. So far I've only needed to carry a child of mine to the car once or twice. Again, it's crucial for a mother to win these battles for control when a child is young and can be physically controlled more easily.

While I was struggling through a difficult pregnancy, I developed the habit of correcting my children from across the room. Once I finally sat down, I didn't want to get up, because I felt as big and uncomfortable as a beached whale. I soon discovered, however, that "remote control" correction is ineffective. Parents must be willing to get up and take action. It didn't take long for my children to start ignoring my long-distance commands. Effective discipline will keep us on our toes.

When an adult gives a command, children will often pause and look at the adult to see if they really mean it. In order to prevent nagging, the adult may need to say firmly, "What did I say?" as they step forward to enforce their words—if necessary. Usually children will obey right away, since they've tested the adult and found she wasn't bluffing.

The desire to have children like us is great, but the desire to do what is best for children must be even greater. My goal as a teacher or parent is not to win a popularity contest, but to teach children about the consequences of their actions. It is important for children to learn that wrong actions have immediate consequences even if it means they'll be unhappy about being punished.

Often, as a teacher, after I punished a student, she would go back to her desk, take out paper and crayons, and draw me a picture of rainbows, hearts, and butterflies with a note that said, "I love you, Miss Johnson." This was because she knew she was breaking our rule and she expected me to follow through. As a result, she respected me more. Of course, I can't guarantee that you'll get a little love note every time you follow through with discipline.

Once a parent or teacher understands these four basic principles: (1) maximizing the trainable years, (2) linking responsibility with privilege, (3) making the punishment match the offense, and (4) following through consistently with punishment, he or she will have the foundation upon which a system of discipline is built and will be ready to deal with preventing discipline problems.

4

Prevention

It's wise to plan ahead and prevent potential discipline problems before they happen. I don't want to give my children or students any chance to disobey, so I make obedience look as exciting and glamorous as possible, while at the same time making disobedience look unappealing.

The following six preventions will encourage children to want to obey. These preventions can work proactively to help minimize discipline conflicts.

Establish Clear Boundaries and Consequences from the Start

In *Dare to Discipline*, Dr. James Dobson tells of the educational trends of the '60s, where freedom was thought to enhance learning and creativity. As a result, one principal saw the fence around his school's playground as an obstacle to freedom, so he removed the fence. Then, an interesting phenomenon occurred: instead of using the entire playground to play, the children huddled in little groups at the center of the playground. The fence wasn't an obstacle to freedom after all; instead,

27

it gave the children a sense of security. It represented protection from outsiders, such as dogs and strangers. They were safe inside the fence, while intruders were kept out.

Firm boundaries give children security. Often children will push up against the fence to see how firm it is. If it holds firm, they feel secure. But if they can push the fence out a little further, they will keep moving it further and further. If boundaries and consequences are established before children disobey, many will not disobey because they know exactly what is expected of them.

On the first day of school, as soon as the children were settled into their seats, I greeted them and gave them our classroom rules. I always started out by saying, "Third grade is a great grade! You're going to learn all sorts of wonderful things this year, like how to multiply and divide, and how to write in cursive. In order to learn all these things and more, you'll need to learn our classroom rules. Now, I'm looking for some good listeners. I want to see how many of you can remember our rules and repeat them back to me when I'm done." Then, before they ever got a chance to disobey, I told them what was expected of them, what rewards they would receive for good behavior, and what penalties they would receive for disobedience. As the students repeated them back to me, I rewarded them for remembering.

For the next couple of days, I would start each morning by asking the children to tell me our rules. This reinforced the rules in their minds. On those first days of school, a few students will always press up against the fence just to see how firm it is. The teacher must show the child that the fence will hold firm. For the first week or two, I needed to work hard at enforcing the rules, but soon the children would settle into our routine and we had fewer problems.

At home, the boundaries and consequences will vary greatly depending on your child's age and ability. With a baby who is on the verge of crawling or walking, you should decide what objects and areas of the house are off-limits before your baby discovers them and creates disaster.

When a child comes over to play with my toddler, I tell both of them our rules about sharing toys. This allows the children to play more cooperatively before any problems break out. When I take one of my sons to a friend's house to play, before we arrive, we discuss how he can be a courteous guest. As my children grow, so do my expectations of them. I strive to keep them informed of new responsibilities.

At several points throughout Scripture, God clearly lays out rules, establishing firm boundaries. In the Garden of Eden, God made it clear that Adam and Eve could eat the fruit from any of the trees except from the tree of the knowledge of good and evil. When Eve spoke to Satan, she reminded him of God's warning that she would die if she ate from it. Once Adam and Eve had both eaten from the tree, God punished them and they spiritually died (Genesis 3).

In Judges 13:5, the angel of the Lord carefully explained to Samson's mother, before he was even born, that he wasn't to cut his hair during his whole life. So long as he lived by this rule, God gave him superhuman strength. Samson knew this rule, and one day when his hair was cut, God remained true to His word. Samson lost his strength and became weak like any other man.

In these passages and many others, God clearly explained what He expected. He set clear boundaries and promised blessings for obedience. He also warned in advance of punishment if they violated His commands. Nothing was random or haphazard. He did not send random lightning bolts out of the sky. When His commands were violated, He followed through with the punishment.

These biblical examples map out the course we are to take as parents and teachers. Following God's example, we must also clearly explain to children what we expect of them. We must set clear boundaries and promise blessing for obedience. We also need to warn of punishment for disobedience. We should never be random or haphazard. When a child disobeys we must follow through with the punishment.

Stop New Trends Before They Get Out of Hand

I always looked for anything that had the potential to create chaos in my classroom. My "radar" was constantly looking for any small action that could get out of control. One time while I was leading children's church, a boy in the middle row put his feet on the back of the chair in front of him. Almost instantly two other children also put their feet up. Nothing bad had happened, but I could see the potential for all kinds of problems. I walked over to the second row, looked at the offending feet and said, "We will keep our feet on the floor in here." End of problem.

At home, I take this prevention one step further by stopping potentially bad habits from developing. At the ripe old age of six months, our first son was quickly becoming attached to his pacifier. We must have had at least five, but they had a way of disappearing whenever we needed them most. One afternoon, my husband and I turned our entire house upside-down looking for that elusive piece of plastic while our son screamed uncontrollably. We knew something needed to be done to prevent future repeat episodes. I determined that a pacifier was too valuable to lose, so the crib became the home of our pacifiers. When I came to claim him at the end of naptime, I would take out his pacifier and leave it in the crib. Eventually, he pulled out his pacifier and dropped it into the crib as I lifted him out.

As he got even older, he took inventory of his stuffed animals before he went to sleep. If one was missing, he became upset. We decided that all his stuffed animals also "lived" in his crib. They waited there for him all day until he came for his nap or bedtime. Not only did this prevent him from losing his stuffed animals, it also kept them much cleaner, since they were no longer dragged all over the house.

Praise Good Behavior in a Warm Atmosphere

If you develop a warm atmosphere of praise and recognition, fewer discipline problems will erupt. Be specific. I tell my sons frequently how pleased I am when they share with one another. In my classroom, certain children frequently got in trouble and I knew I needed to really concentrate on catching them behaving nicely. They desperately needed some positive recognition. Then

31

there were the children who tended to blend in with the background. They also needed positive recognition or one day they might act out in negative ways just to be noticed.

When I made a specific effort to praise the first two or three students who had their books and paper out for the next topic and were waiting quietly, the general hubbub of my classroom dropped and the other students began rushing to take out their books and paper as well. But on days when I ignored the few quiet ones, and focused on making all of the noisy ones quiet, I often ended up chasing from one noisy group to the next while the quiet ones started to fidget and grow restless. This became an exercise in futility. It was more effective to focus my attention on those who were doing right than on those who were not.

At home, I can praise my children individually, but there is not a group of children around to give them a lot of recognition. Whenever possible, I praise my child in front of his siblings. I say, "My, how big you are! You set the table all by yourself. The baby wishes he could set the table and be big like you." Then when Daddy comes home from work, I tell him of our son's accomplishment, praising him in front of Daddy so he can bask in the limelight.

A major part of a warm atmosphere is developing a special relationship with each child. Even with 27 students, I tried hard to see each child as an individual and to build a unique relationship with each one. *Female* teachers of elementary children can put an arm around the child's shoulder, tousle a child's hair, or hug a child. All of these actions say, "I like you" to a child. When my students walked in line, I often held hands with the child at the end of the line, which also enabled me to watch the whole line. When I walked across the playground, I had a ready smile or encouraging word for any student I met. During the day, if a child expressed concern about something, I shared the concern. I also joked with my students and we enjoyed laughing together. The more I developed individual relationships with the children, the more they were ready to obey, because they knew I genuinely cared for each one.

At home we establish a warm atmosphere by waking the children affectionately and cheerfully. I usually greet each one by saying, "Good morning, Sunshine!" and then give him a big hug. Our day is heavily seasoned with laughter, hugs, and kisses. I constantly look for opportunities to encourage each child individually. We always end the day cozily as we read to them, sing to them, and give them each a kiss. We often pray, thanking God for a great day and asking for His protection all night long. Over the years, I've developed a personal lullaby for each child. I use the tune of a familiar lullaby, like "Rock-a-bye Baby," and create new words about my child. The boys love their special lullabies. All of these things help create a loving home atmosphere where a child feels secure. If a child feels secure and receives ample positive attention, the child will not need to act up to receive negative attention from the parents.

Avoid Idleness and Boredom

Both of these invite trouble. Idle children will find mischief. In the classroom, I always made sure to keep the lessons moving at a quick pace. This guaranteed that the students did not have time to even think about getting in trouble. Transitions from one topic to another also need to move swiftly. If there is any idle time, the children will gladly fill it for the teacher. But the teacher may not be very happy with the way they choose to fill it!

To prevent idle time and boredom, I always came to school at least an hour early to prepare for the day. Folding papers, writing the daily routine on the chalkboard, making copies, etc., was all done before the students walked in the door. While they were in my care, I gave them all my attention. I never assumed that recess time would be mine later in the day, since often something unexpected would come up and rob me of that time. If I did have any free time at recess, I used it to grade papers or do some future planning—like planning for the next day.

Idle time and boredom also lead to trouble at home. While riding in the car, especially on long road trips, my sons bring along some car toys. When we have to sit and wait at the doctor's office, I encourage them to play hide-and-seek behind the chairs and under the tables in the waiting room. Often other children, who are also bored, end up joining us, too. Helping my boys to focus on an exciting activity cuts down on the amount of fighting. Now they're starting to create their own adventures and excitement while playing together.

Establish a Schedule

In the classroom, we always had the same basic schedule. This gave the children predictability and security. They knew what to anticipate as the day unfolded. They always started the day by getting out a piece of paper and a pencil. Then they quietly began working on their first topic of the day. I walked around their desks, quietly rewarding the students who were working. Some children would be halfway through their lesson while others were just settling in.

In establishing a classroom schedule, a teacher must make sure that basic academic subjects like spelling, math, reading, and writing are taught before lunch, when the children's minds are fresh. In the afternoon, children are not as bright and alert, so this is a good time for art, music, physical education, science, and social studies. Younger children have shorter attention spans, so the quiet independent work times will be much shorter for kindergartners or first graders. A teacher is also wise to vary the day with direct instruction to the whole class, small-group work time, and quiet independent work time.

Just as a schedule is necessary to establish an orderly classroom, so it is necessary to establish an orderly home. Because my children know their daily routine, naptime and bedtime do not turn into major conflicts. I read them stories, sing them songs, kiss them, and then they go to sleep. No whining and no questions asked because this is always the routine. I want to make bedtime a pleasant experience. The only time it ever turned into a battlefield, was when each child graduated from their crib to a bed. Suddenly, there were no boundaries surrounding the bed and newfound freedom was calling. In the first week or two, we had many conflicts, sometimes four or five a night. We didn't give up, and eventually each child learned to stay on his bed until morning.

In establishing our home schedule, as soon as possible after each baby was born, I tried to get the baby on a schedule compatible with the family schedule. Over the months, the baby's schedule gradually became more and more like the family schedule. Obviously, a breast-fed baby did not nurse while we were having meals, but once the baby started to eat solids, he ate them when we ate. I also worked to align all four of the children's naps at the same time. This naptime gives me two hours of peace and sanity every afternoon. As my older children outgrow the need to nap, they still have a quiet time with books, puzzles, or Lincoln Logs in their room.

Schedules are meant to provide order and predictability to both children and adults—they also provide sanity for adults. There will be days, like field trip days or vacation days, when a schedule may become too cumbersome to keep. There's no need to become legalistic about a schedule. Instead, use a schedule on a regular basis, to provide continuity.

Express Excitement and Children Will Want to Learn

If I'm convinced that the topic I'm teaching is important, then the children will catch that excitement, too. By my tone of voice and facial expressions, the students can tell if I'm genuinely interested in the topic. I can draw them in by using dramatic pauses and creating a level of anticipation. The more "real" I make a topic by showing pictures, doing an experiment, giving them something to touch, the more I capture their interest.

During a lesson on condensation and the water cycle, for example, I encouraged my students to go home and ask to see the inside of a lid when their mother was cooking dinner. I explained that the inside should be covered with water droplets or condensed steam. The next morning, Marcus came to class and told me breathlessly how he had counted 55 drops of water on his lid! If dinnertime at his house is anything like at my house, I could easily picture him standing in the middle of his kitchen floor carefully counting each drop while his mother frantically tried to cook dinner around him.

Another day, I introduced a unit on the solar system and briefly told the students what we would be learning. The next morning, Aaron told me he had gone home and read about Saturn in his encyclopedia. He eagerly started quoting interesting facts.

The parent's interest in the child's education can have a major impact on the child's desire to learn and participate. When our son came home from Sunday School each week, he would tell me who he played with at recess, but I could not get him to tell me about the Bible story. One day his teacher said he was a distraction during the story time. At that point, I decided that asking him about his story was not enough. I warned him of future punishment if he became a distraction again.

The next week before he went to Sunday School, I asked him to pay close attention to his story so he could tell me all about it on our way home in the van. I also reminded him of punishment if he became a distraction. As soon as we pulled out of the church parking lot, I eagerly asked him to tell me his story. Each week the stories became more and more detailed, and I knew he was listening better because I was expressing interest before and after Sunday School.

Our younger son needed practice developing his drawing skills, so each week I expressed great interest in whatever he made in Sunday School. As I picked him up, I was delighted with whatever he made. Soon when I arrived to pick him up, he would run to me with a smile and say, "Mommy, look at what I made!"

At home, children are keenly aware of what is interesting to their parents. If the parents take time to include the child in their hobbies or interests, the child may develop a lifelong pastime, which can then be shared with the parent.

5

Ages and Expectations

As children grow and move to different levels of development, a wise teacher or parent should set realistic expectations for a child based on his or her current developmental level. If the adult sets the expectations too low, the child will become spoiled, lazy, or dependent. If the adult sets the expectations too high, the child will either become an overachiever who is never satisfied, or he will become exasperated and give up. Let's look at some ways to set reasonable expectations.

Since a teacher usually has a classroom filled with children of the same age, she will quickly see the wide range of normal development for her group of students. The curriculum she uses will also help her set reasonable expectations on the behavior of her students.

A parent's job isn't so easy. Since parents have a child for their lifetime, they will just get used to dealing with one level of development, only to see their child move on to a new level, requiring them to adjust their expectations, responses, and rules again. Multiple siblings, all of differing ages and abilities, can keep the parent in a constant state of uncertainty. Sometimes, the only thing that really seems sure in life is change.

Through careful observation, however, parents can become experts about their child. They'll come to know each child's strengths and weaknesses. They'll know their child's likes and dislikes. They'll know their child's basic personality type and how to motivate each one. They should also notice basic patterns of behavior that could be the seeds of an emerging bad habit.

All of this should serve as the backdrop for setting realistic expectations for a child's behavior. As a parent recognizes a child's current developmental level, whether it be intellectual, physical, or social, she should set expectations that align with the child's level.

Since I'm in the midst of raising four children, I've been fascinated to see this process of development unfold before my eyes. Some children have been early talkers, articulating beautiful, clear sentences long before most of their peers. At the same time their gross motor skills, like walking, were slower. Other children were early walkers, but slow talkers. This could have been very alarming, but I've noticed a pattern. Rarely does a child develop on all levels at the same time. Often he develops early in one area and late in another. Understanding this will reduce a parent's concern about a child's development in comparison to an advanced peer, and help to set realistic expectations for a child's behavior based on a child's current level of development.

Toddlers

Over the centuries, two-year-olds have earned the title "terrible twos." Regardless of the personality of the child—or the parent, for that matter—the child will inevitably enter this phase. The length and severity of this stage will vary from child to child.

The "terrible twos" usually start around 18 months and end around 30 months (or 2 1/2 years). During this time a child tries to establish his own identity. A battle of the wills may erupt when the toddler seeks to pursue his own agenda.

At this stressful time of life, a wise parent will look for signs of understanding to determine a child's intellectual ability. A child will hear and understand language before he will be able to speak. A child's listening vocabulary will always be higher than his speaking vocabulary. If he demonstrates understanding when the parent speaks about another cup of juice, or playing with a new toy, or putting an object in another room, then he can be expected to obey simple, clear commands. Using gestures along with words will increase a child's understanding.

Often children in the midst of this challenging stage are allowed to get away with inappropriate behavior. The parent has made the false assumption that, "He doesn't understand what he is doing. It wouldn't be fair to punish him if he doesn't understand." Sadly, most toddlers understand far more than most adults give them credit for. As a result, these children may take more and more liberty bending and breaking rules as they go.

Once a month, I work in the nursery with children in the 14 to 20 month age group. I talk to early toddlers and expect them to respond. They do. I'll ask a child to get a book so I can read him a story. He will go to the bookshelf, select a book and bring it to me. Often, other nursery workers are amazed at the level of understanding

41

these little ones demonstrate. All they need is to have someone talk to them, not at them. Then they need someone who will encourage them to stretch to new heights in a fun environment.

As a child consistently demonstrates understanding, then it is fair to expect him to obey simple commands. These commands should always be linked to areas where he has already shown competence. Make learning new skills a fun game, as a child shows he can do something on a predictable basis, later it would be fair to expect him to obey in that area. A parent's tone of voice can communicate the difference between a game and a command.

At some point during this stage, all of my children have played the *Yes/No Game*. I first noticed it one evening when my oldest son, who was two at the time, couldn't make up his mind about whether or not he wanted to go outside and play. I was running around the kitchen trying to fix dinner. I opened the door. He stepped out onto the back porch and I shut the door and resumed cooking. He stood there and started fussing. I went back to the door, opened it and let him in. Then I went back to my dinner preparation while he stood at the door looking out. He started fussing to get out, but once I opened the door, he changed his mind. This became very frustrating as my dinner preparation ground to a halt. I knew I needed to resolve this. Since he wasn't strong enough to open our door, I left the door slightly open and told him he could come in or go out. He still stood there at the door, but I made it clear that I would focus on dinner and not the door.

This frustrating *Yes/No Game* would crop up at unexpected times during the day. Sometimes, during our bedtime ritual, he told me that he didn't want me to read him a bedtime story. Then I put the story down and he protested, claiming he did want a story. I reminded him that he just said he didn't want a story. He insisted on a story, so I got the book, only to have him say he didn't want a story. Some days he would play this same game with the song that was also a part of our ritual.

As this became more and more frustrating, I knew I needed a permanent solution to this game that wouldn't go away. One day as he started to play *Yes/No* about his story, I said, "Fine. You will have no story today." I got up, put the book back on the shelf and returned to his bedside. "I won't play the *Yes/No Game* with you. You said you didn't want a story, now you won't get one." He became frantic, begging me to read him a story. I told him he could have a story tomorrow. He lost control and started screaming. I told him that he had already lost his story, but if he could control himself I would still sing him a song. He was so distraught, he said he didn't want a song. So I told him that the next day I would read him a story and sing him a song, but he had lost these privileges for today. He went ballistic, sobbing and carrying on. I calmly walked out of the room and shut the door.

As soon as I had a strategy for dealing with this, he quickly gave up playing the game. Now when my oldest sees younger siblings test their independence and start playing the game, he shakes his head and says, "We don't play the *Yes/No Game* in this family." As a result the children are learning to say what they mean and mean what they say.

More expectations should be placed on a child as he matures. If a child is an only child or has a large age gap between him and the next sibling, a parent may have the time-luxury of putting on all of his clothes for him, or feeding him each bite of food. In our home, because my last three children were born in the span of 3 years, as a matter of survival I graduated children from cribs to big beds long before their second birthday. They also graduated from their highchair at an early age to make way for the baby. Because I was in a survival mode, I was eager to teach each child basic self-help skills, like dressing or putting up their dirty dishes, as soon as they could.

The more I allowed them to do, the more they increased in confidence and self-respect, and the less stressed I was about all the little things so I could focus more on being a mommy and pouring my love on them.

If you're struggling with all of the demands of taking care of several small children at the same time, don't feel guilty about off-loading some tasks onto the children. Always look for little things they can do to contribute to the needs of themselves or the family. As you involve them, they'll take pride in being mommy's big helper, and you'll be off-loading some of the tremendous burden mothers of young children carry. Your child doesn't need a full-time maid. He needs a mommy to nurture him, and he needs self-confidence that he too can contribute to making his family better.

Preschoolers

We live in an age of choices. Adults want freedom to make choices. Responsible adults have earned the right to make all types of choices from diet to occupation and home.

A child's view of the world around him is very limited; as a result, he needs a foundation of basic facts before he is prepared to make wise choices. If a preschooler were given total freedom to choose whatever food he wanted for each meal, the average child would select chips, cookies, soda pop, and candy.

A wise adult will always start by giving a child a solid model of healthy nutrition. After the child develops a taste for healthy food, the adult may gradually allow the child some freedom between healthy choices. Does he want carrots or cucumbers with his sandwich? He might also have dessert after eating a reasonable serving of food.

This principle of providing a solid model to serve as a base for good future choices is true in every area of life. A preschooler should first learn the correct way to do something, like taking turns or sharing. If he's left in a situation with another child, but neither has been shown how to be fair and take turns, they'll end up "working it out." This usually means the law of the jungle will prevail. One child dominates while another defers. Neither has learned about fairness and taking turns. Instead, one has learned to use force to get his way, while the other has learned that he has no rights. It is far better to first give children guidelines of fair play before they have a dispute. Then when the dispute arises, help them to make fair choices.

Children at this age need lots of repetition, so don't expect them to remember a day or two later. Once a preschooler is given a model for good nutrition, fair play and so many other areas of life, he'll grow up with a solid foundation upon which to build wise decisions as he moves on to the elementary years and the greater choices that lie beyond.

Reasoning Ability

A preschooler is a concrete thinker. That's why they say cute things that charm adults. The world for them is only concrete reality. Abstract reasoning or thought is a higher function that usually develops in the child's seventh or eighth year.

Thus abstract concepts like *the United States*, *independence*, or *jealousy* are difficult for a concrete thinker to grasp. If you want to communicate an abstract truth to a preschooler, you must make it as concrete as possible. The more you use tangible objects to describe the intangible, the better your chances of communication. Stories like *Aesop's Fables* are excellent for communicating abstract truth. If your child "get's it," that's great.

But keep in mind that you may still try to push your children beyond their ability to understand. If they don't understand you, drop it. One day they will understand, but until then, they shouldn't be made to feel stupid or rebellious.

Imagination

At this stage of life, children's imaginations can be a powerful influence. They should be allowed to develop their imaginations through playing. Children often learn to deal with problems from the real world by acting them out in their play world. A child who picks up a stick and shoots at imaginary bad guys, may be building confidence to deal with a real bully at preschool.

The line between imagination and reality may blur at times in the mind of a preschooler. Don't take everything they say at full value. My three-year-old can tell wild tales about the scrape on his knee, and with each telling the details change. I don't call him a liar or make an issue of it.

When he has broken a rule, I talk with him seriously and ask for all the details. He knows lying will be punished.

There are rare times when an adult should be concerned about a child's imagination. If the child spends more waking hours in isolated imaginary play, than he does with any other activity, the parent or teacher should encourage the child to socialize more. Of even greater concern is the child who cruelly maims or dismembers an animal like a bird or squirrel. The adult should investigate the matter fully, and make sure the child doesn't commit any future acts of violence.

Gestures

The use of gestures is a standard form of communication between adults. Preschoolers, however, won't pick them up through osmosis. They must be taught them.

Often when I am either talking with someone in person or on the phone, I'll try to communicate to my preschoolers through hand gestures so I won't have to interrupt the conversation. Most often I'm trying to tell them to stop doing whatever they're doing—like making noise or grabbing something they shouldn't have. Pushing their hand away often isn't enough. I usually end up getting frustrated, which interrupts the conversation further. It's taken me a long time to realize that I need to sit down with my preschoolers during a quiet time when there are no distractions and train them about gestures that mean stop, or no, or wait a minute. Expecting them to read my mind, or decipher my actions is not fair—first I must make sure they understand.

6
Rules for the Classroom and Home

In every city across our land, there are basic laws to protect the best interests of each citizen. These laws protect individual freedom so long as the freedom doesn't infringe on the rights of another and endangers no one. If the laws are fair and consistently enforced, the citizens can freely move about in peace.

This chapter provides home and classroom rules that foster an individual freedom that doesn't infringe on the rights or safety of others. If these rules are fair and are enforced consistently, the children will freely move about in peace and harmony. At the same time, these rules will equip children for adulthood and instill self-control.

Before discussing specific rules, it is worthwhile reviewing three basic principles you should follow when you "lay down the law."

1. Expect Obedience.

Whenever a teacher or parent gives children rules, he or she must expect the children to obey. The adult's manner and tone of voice will speak louder than the actual words used. If a parent gently asks a child to go to bed, chances are good the child will do anything else but go to bed. One father told me about a time he was out of town on business. The mother had tried three times unsuccessfully to tell her son to go to bed. When the father called, he told the son to go bed. The son climbed into bed. The mother watched in amazement. Then she told her husband, "You are over 2,000 miles away, but he obeys you the first time. I'm right here, but he won't obey me." The difference between the two parents was in their expectations. One expected immediate obedience, which was revealed through the tone of voice. While the other was used to saying something over and over, and didn't expect immediate obedience.

2. Specify the consequences for broken rules.

Just as speed limits are useless unless they are reinforced with officers who dispense tickets, so rules are useless unless they are reinforced with rewards and punishments. Teachers and parents need to select appropriate rewards and punishments to go with each rule. Examples of rewards and punishments are covered in the next three chapters.

3. Back up the rules with action.

Not only should you state the consequence, you should also carry out your word. Only give children rules if you expect obedience and are willing to back up the rules with action. Kids are masters at reading adults, and know when an adult means it or not.

Now, let's look at specific home and classroom rules. We first begin with the classroom.

Classroom Rules

Since children come to school to learn, classroom rules should enhance the learning environment. An atmosphere of chaos quickly undermines the best-prepared lesson. A teacher must first establish an atmosphere of control and order. Once this is done, the children are free to focus on learning about all the fascinating topics the teacher has to share with them.

An orderly classroom has two main characteristics the noise level is controlled and the children's actions are controlled. Following are four rules that help maintain order:

1. Only one person talks at a time.

I always told my students, "This means that when I talk, all of you get to listen. When it is Suzie's turn to talk, we all get to listen to her." I wanted to establish a level of mutual respect in the classroom. Often an outspoken student would not hesitate to interrupt a shy student who was speaking. When this happened, I quickly stopped the outspoken student and asked who had permission to speak. Then I had the outspoken child apologize to the shy child in front of the class. This built up the shy student, giving him or her confidence to speak. It also sent a message to all the other shy children that the classroom was a safe place to speak up. When they talked people would listen.

2. Raise your hand to receive permission.

This rule helps to regulate who gets to speak and when and helps to maintain order in the classroom.

51

Whenever a student blurted out an answer, I would remind him that he forgot our rule. Then I would call on a student with a raised hand, saying, "Sharon, I'm so glad you remembered to raise your hand."

3. Keep hands and feet to yourself.

This rule prevents a host of other problems like hitting, pushing, kicking, pinching, and hair pulling. It is especially helpful when children are forming a line. If a student breaks this rule, he instantly forfeits 10 minutes of recess. If a child was hurt, he also needs to apologize, and may face a stiffer penalty.

4. You get only one warning.

This rule serves as a great deterrent. If a child was disruptive while I was leading the class, I stopped in mid-sentence, looked the child in the eye, and said, "That's your warning. Next time you'll lose recess," which was usually 5 or 10 minutes. Most often the child became quite somber and tried very hard to keep from losing precious recess time.

As I shared the above list of rules with the students, I expounded on each one. These rules may also be posted on the wall to serve as a constant reminder.

I don't like giving children too many rules. Rules become cumbersome to enforce and are difficult for children to remember. Some rules, such as turning in neat work or putting your name on your paper, can be stressed in the realm of academics since they have little to do with classroom discipline.

At times when the children were having free time and the noise level got too high, I said, "Attend" in a loud, clear voice. This meant to stop, look, and listen. It usually established order quickly. I made a game of it with the students. They knew when I said, "Attend," I would be looking for the very first ones to respond. As soon as the first two or three children stopped what they were doing and looked up, they were rewarded with a sticker or a point in our discipline system.

After getting the attention of most of the students, I proceeded with the directions for our next activity, speaking in a very soft voice. This forced the rest of the students who were still settling down to stop and listen, or miss out and not know what to do.

Home Rules

While the classroom has one main goal—to be a learning environment— the home has many goals and is the place where we live. As a result, rules for the home are much broader in scope. Home is the place where a family settles in and feels comfortable. Just as we all enjoy different flavors of ice cream, so we all feel comfortable in different home environments. The following rules are given as suggestions to help you decide what fits in your household, and makes your home life less stressful and more enjoyable.

In deciding on new rules that will bring order and peace to your home, you should begin by identifying trouble spots. For example, if your children have certain habits that cause a lot of stress or arguments at certain times—such as bedtime or mealtime, then these trouble spots should receive top priority. The parents should go out to dinner without the children, or discuss the trouble spots after the children are tucked in bed for the night. They need to focus on the specific problem with the specific child and make a plan to deal with it. Parents need to establish rules they know they can enforce. They must be sure to be consistent and follow through every time the rule is obeyed by giving a reward, and every time it is broken by giving the punishment.

After charting a plan of action, the parents need to talk to the child, or children, about the new rule that is going into effect. The child needs to repeat back to the parents the new rule, reward, and punishment he or she will receive. This is done to mark a definite starting point. It should also be done when the child is calm and rational and not in the midst of an angry power struggle. Once the child has mastered this trouble spot, then the parents can move on to implement other house rules. It's always best to focus on only one or two problem areas at a time, and then move on to the others. It's too stressful to try to break five or six bad habits all at the same time.

In talking with numerous parents, some basic areas of home life emerged as trouble spots that created a high level of stress and discipline problems. The following rules deal with those basic areas of home life; including safety, courtesy and sharing, bedtime, mealtime, noise level, getting dressed, tantrums, troop movement, neatness, homework, and other children.

Safety

First and most important, a home needs to be safe. With children under the age of three, the safety risk is the greatest. All the safety plugs and latches should be in place. Small children, especially before they can speak, are at the greatest risk of danger. Telling them of danger will have very little impact, but a firm "No!" while moving the child away, will usually communicate to the child that there is the possibility of harm in what they were about to do.

I don't allow my children to jump off staircases or furniture. As each of my sons began to crawl and wanted to get down off a bed or out of a chair, I would turn him around on his stomach with his feet pointing over the edge then I would gently ease him down until his feet touched the floor. Soon they each did this on their own.

I began training them on the stairs in the same way, one step at a time. This usually frustrated my toddlers while they were learning because they couldn't see where they were going. Once they got the hang of it, however, they loved their newfound freedom as they safely crawled up the stairs on their stomachs, and slid down feet first on their stomachs.

Courtesy and Sharing

When there is more than one child in the family, basic rules of courtesy are essential. Our children are not allowed to hit or kick each other. This rule comes with a serious punishment. They are not allowed to speak unkindly to each other or call one another names. When it comes to sharing a toy, the child who was playing with it first gets to play with it. If the owner of the toy decides he wants to play with it, he can't just take it away. Instead he says, "I want to play with my toy. So in two minutes it will be my turn." The first child has been warned. This gives him two more minutes to enjoy the truck and prepare to give it back. When his time is up, relinquishing the toy is easier, while the owner says, "Thank you." A simple kitchen timer is ideal for ticking off the time.

I draw the line on sharing special stuffed animals or blankets. Those belong to a specific child who should not be forced to share them. If the child chooses to share, that is different. Since my children's animals and blankets stay on their beds, this dilemma rarely arises.

When a child is young, he or she needs to learn the rules of common courtesy and fair play. Parents often need to intervene to make sure that all is fair. Otherwise, the law of the jungle prevails—the bigger, stronger child will always get his way. As children learn common courtesy, they gradually begin to treat each other fairly and a parent's intervention is needed less and less.

Bedtime

From the time our children were babies, we've made bedtime a pleasant experience. Bedtime is always at the same time. This is maintained unless we are out and cannot get home sooner. By having a consistent bedtime, a child's own little body clock is also winding down and he or she is ready to go to sleep. The child knows he always goes to bed at the same time, so he rarely tries to negotiate, because the rule never changes. The bedtime ritual starts by putting on pajamas. We then read a story and sing at least one song to each child as we tuck them into bed with a prayer and a kiss. When our children were very young, they also had a bottle or cup before bed, which stopped when a child graduated from the crib to a big bed. In the excitement of now sleeping in a big bed, the child never missed the cup. This also made potty training and nighttime dryness easier to accomplish.

Once the children are in bed, two other rules go into effect.

1. No getting out of bed.

For us, our big bedtime battles occurred when our children were transitioning from the crib to a big bed.

Suddenly, there were no boundaries surrounding them. Those first few nights we often had four or five battles a night, but we consistently followed through and punished every time. Soon, the child settled in and bedtime was once again pleasant.

Unless a child genuinely has to go to the bathroom—and we made sure the child really went—there is no getting out of bed. One son could manage to go three or four times at 20-minute intervals. We put a stop to that by telling him he had to go once and make sure he was all done, because the second time he would be punished. This can usually be eliminated by making sure all drinks stop an hour before bedtime, and by making sure a child uses the bathroom right before going to bed.

2. No loud talking.

We do allow the children to whisper as long as we don't hear it. I believe some kind of special bonding happens between children who whisper and share secrets in the dark. I want my children to be as close to each other as possible.

My neighbor's children share a room. Some nights she can hear them quietly discussing the BIG questions of life. Questions like, "What makes a volcano erupt?" She knows these private talks strengthen their friendship.

Since a child is already in bed, it is often difficult to think of an appropriate punishment for bedtime violations. My friend, Cathy, has an effective penalty for her children. If one of them talks loudly or gets out of bed, she puts the offender on *time out*. The child has to sit out in the hall. This has been very effective as her son will sit in the hall looking dejected. When time is up, he gladly returns to his cozy bed ready to sleep.

Mealtime

Getting our children to eat their food is a never-ending battle. To minimize the stress, I started training them when they were babies. From the first time I introduced solid foods to my babies, I gave them the least tasty food first while they were hungriest. After it was gone, or mostly gone, I introduced the tastier food, which had been placed strategically out of sight. This was an attempt to broaden each child's taste for food. With preschool children, I put a reasonable portion of meat and vegetables on their plate first. After this is eaten, they're free to fill up on the starch—mashed potatoes or bread—and anything else on the menu. Our children get dessert only if they successfully eat the food we have given them. We make sure they eat a minimum number of bites, but if they choose not to eat all of their meal, they're dismissed without any starches or dessert. They're also told they will only have water, no snacks or juice or milk, until the next meal. This way there's no nagging. We let hunger dictate.

One mother gives her child a piece of bread—he enjoys it better than dessert—if he eats at least one bite of everything on his plate.

Another mother came up with the perfect cure for children who complain about the food. If her children complain, she quietly takes away their plate, and gives them just a glass of water. They all know the rule, and she doesn't nag them or warn them.

We also enforce basic highchair etiquette in our home. Spitting food and dropping food on the floor are not allowed. This has carried over, as our children have grown, to develop proper manners at the table.

Noise Level

Some people can get a lot accomplished in a noisy environment. I cannot. As a result, the noise level in our home is important to me. Angry screaming and yelling is never allowed. The noise level is kept moderate. Happy squealing that comes during play is allowed. But we are working to keep it down when Mom is on the phone.

It's very frustrating to try and carry on a conversation with someone who is in another room. As a result, we make sure we are in the same room if we are going to talk. The only times we yell in the house are if someone is wanted on the phone or at the door, or if a meal is ready. Ideally, instead of having to yell, a child will be nearby and will serve as the messenger, running to each person and telling them dinner is ready.

We rarely watch television, but when we do, it's turned off as soon as we've finished watching. We don't leave it droning on as background noise. Uplifting music, however, can set a soothing background.

Getting Dressed

A parent rejoices as a child becomes more capable and independent and can finally dress herself. The novelty of this new skill often wears off, however, and a child decides she no longer wants to dress herself—or at least not on Mom's time schedule. It's easiest for me to dress our children as soon as they get out of bed. Since the boys share a bedroom, I help the younger child while the older ones dress themselves. Every morning I say to the younger child, "Do you think we can beat the big kids today?" Then the race is on as they hurry to see who can get dressed first. When the last sock is pulled on, we race downstairs to eat breakfast.

For some reason, my children haven't tired of this game. It also works at bedtime when they are putting on their pajamas. If your children stubbornly refuse to get dressed in a reasonable amount of time, you should lay out their clothes for the day, set a timer, and if they don't get done in time, have an appropriate punishment preselected. A natural consequence could be forfeiting breakfast. They can remain in their room dressing while the family is eating breakfast. Another natural consequence could be sending them to school in their pajamas, or whatever they are wearing when the timer rings—within reason, of course. They chose not to dress, and thus chose to go to school and be embarrassed—in the section on rebellion, there is a true story about this.

Tantrums

Since temper tantrums are socially unacceptable, I want my boys to learn that they will get nowhere when they throw one. As soon as one of my sons throws himself down on the ground, starts banging his head on the floor, or just starts screaming in protest, I calmly but firmly tell him we don't want to listen to all his noise. He is sent to a quiet, empty room all by himself until he calms down. He is free to join the family whenever he has cooled off and adjusted his attitude. Often an angry child will need to be carried to the quiet room.

This process even worked when my child was one-year old. The minute he started to throw a fit, I picked him up and said, "When you can be quiet, Mommy will come and get you." I repeated this two or three times emphasizing the word *quiet*. I put him in an empty playpen in another room and left the door slightly ajar. As soon as the screaming stopped, I went in and got him, saying, "Oh, it's so nice and quiet!" By this time, his whole attitude was different. I lifted him out and hugged him, telling him again how quiet he was. He learned the meaning of quiet very quickly.

After a few episodes like this, whenever he started to work himself into a tantrum, I picked him up to carry him into the next room. When I did, his whole attitude would change and he would become quiet before we even reached the playpen. When this happened, he was free to go on playing.

Dealing with temper tantrums while a child is very young is much easier than dealing with an older child who is stronger, more stubborn, and more sophisticated.

Troop Movement

A major stress for me has been moving my crew of small children from point A to point B with all the diaper bags, my purse, and any extra paraphernalia. This was especially stressful when I was pregnant and had a hard time just moving me! The later I am, the more stressed I become. On cold or rainy days, I know I need to allow myself more time so I can get the kids all bundled up in their jackets.

Once again, friendly competition has helped me move my crew more efficiently. As we get ready to go, I mention that the baby—whom I still have to carry at this point—is going to beat them out to the van. This is the ultimate challenge—they don't want to be outdone by a baby! By the time baby and I reach the van, we are greeted by children who have climbed into their seats and are chanting, "We beat you, we beat you!" I always tell them that next time the baby will win.

One mother gives the first child to the car the privilege of putting the key in the door lock. The kids are eager to rush to the car because of this simple reward.

Getting out of the car in a busy parking lot with multiple children in tow can also be very dangerous. I have taught them to stand next to our van and wait until I am done getting the baby out—they all have a healthy fear of moving cars and busy streets. When we move through the parking lot to the building, we all hold hands and they stay close to me. No running is allowed—*ever!*

Neatness

This area will vary the most from home to home. Both parents should agree on a comfortable standard of clean. Inevitably, once children join the family, the ideal level of clean becomes harder to maintain. Often parents will need to set a new standard between their ideal and reality. If a mother wants to keep an impeccable house all the time, she will inevitably devote less of her time and energy to her children and more to the house. Her children may grow up feeling unimportant and resentful of the house. A wise, mature mother once told me not to sweat the little things with my children or they might grow up too meticulous and inhibited.

How can a parent establish reasonable rules for the right balance between neatness and comfort? This arena of neatness encompasses two subcategories: cutting off a mess at the source, before it spreads; and establishing an orderly system for storing toys, and everything else.

First, let's look at some ways to cut off a mess at the source. Surprisingly, many of the answers do not come from our "American way." One example of this occurred while we were living in Berlin. We became friends with people from several different countries. I noticed that many of these people immediately took off their shoes upon entering our home. One woman always carried a pair of slippers in her bag and would put them on as she entered someone's home. This custom makes a lot of sense. Now all my children take off their shoes as soon as they come in the front door, or when they come in from the backyard. This cuts down on the mess they can track through our home and it helps prolong the life of our carpet.

We also have a policy on food and drinks—no food is "to go." Meals are always eaten at the table. Snacks and drinks are either taken outside in nice weather, or the children sit on their special "juice stool" until they've finished. This stool is in the kitchen on the "easy to clean" tile floor. If they choose to get up and walk around with their snack or drink, they lose it, and don't get any more food until the next meal. If a child spills on the floor or makes a mess, we clean it up together. Most often, it's an accident and not an act of disobedience. As long as it's not disobedience, we clean up the mess and nothing more is said about it.

This policy of a child cleaning up his own mess also applies to all of the messes my kids create. They know if they make a mess with their toys, it's their job to pick it up. As a result, they think twice before making a mess.

Second, when a parent establishes an orderly system for the children's toys, books, clothes, and shoes, the child can take great pride in putting something back where it belongs. Not only will this keep the house neater, it will also prevent them from losing so many things.

A friend, Sherry, grew more frustrated each time her daughter lost a shoe. Often when they were ready to hurry out the door, they ended up hunting for the lost shoe. By the time it was found, they were late and everyone's nerves were shot. Then one day she thought of the perfect solution. She put a large basket at the front door. This became the shoe basket.

Whenever I find myself wishing for the perfectly meticulous model home, I remind myself that one day our nest will be empty and I'll have lots of time for maintaining a gorgeous house. Right now, for me, my energy supply is better spent on my children.

Homework

If a child is struggling with homework, the parents need to establish a system of daily contact with the child's teacher. A simple way to do this is with a steno notebook. The child should write down all the daily assignments and check them off as each item is completed. The unchecked items become homework. The teacher needs to sign the bottom of the page to verify that the child's list is accurate. A parent will also sign the bottom of the page once the homework is done. Both parent and teacher are free to further communicate through this book as the need arises.

As the habit is starting, the teacher and parents should remind the child; but the goal is to have the child take full responsibility for completing the work as soon as possible. If the child forgets, the teacher should make sure the child has the notebook and the day's homework before leaving the school grounds. Once at home, the child should have a quick snack and review the directions for the homework with the parent to make sure the child understands what to do. Then the child should go to the designated homework station—a well-lit corner of a quiet room with a desk and chair—and begin to work.

Depending on the child's age and attention span, the child should work at 10, 15, or 20-minute intervals, pausing so a parent can check the work to make sure the child is on the right track. A kitchen timer works great for keeping track of the work time. The goal is to make the intervals longer and longer, until the child completes the homework alone and has a parent merely check to see that it is done. During the short breaks when the parent comes to check the work, the child is free to stand and stretch. The child should be encouraged to work accurately. Once the child can work accurately, then the child should work on speed, striving to complete the work in less time.

The child should be rewarded for any completed homework and should remain in the homework station, if choosing to move slowly, until the work is done. If this doesn't work and the child allows the work to drag on and on, then try a different penalty. Usually, the lure of free time to run and play in the yard or with neighbors is enough to encourage most children to get their homework done. This is discussed further in the chapter on punishment.

Other Children

When other children come into your home, it's reasonable for you to expect them to abide by your house rules. This can be difficult if the children's mother is with them and is not supportive. If this is the case, you do have a right to step in and prevent a child from hurting your home, your property, or your child. If their mother isn't present, then you have more freedom in establishing your house rules. In either setting, merely say, "In our house, we have this rule . . ." Be firm and matter of fact.

Let the child know what he or she can expect for breaking the rule.

This principle can extend beyond the walls of your home. If you're at the park, or anywhere else, and another child comes up and threatens to harm your child, you have a right to intervene if you don't think your child feels comfortable defending himself or herself.

The above house rules are general suggestions for dealing with potential problem areas. Once you've decided what rules you want to set up in your own home, you'll need to select specific rewards and punishments for many of the rules. Some of these ideas, however, may not need a reward or punishment, like leaving shoes at the door, because they're habits and the children do it regardless of whether they like it or not.

When children are told new rules, they need to hear of any rewards or punishments right from the start. Choosing a fair punishment is much easier when it is selected during a calm period, as opposed to waiting until the heat of the moment when you may not be as rational.

At all times, remember to set rules that are appropriate for the age and skill level of each child. As a child develops, some rules will phase out while others will phase in.

7
Rewards

Rewards motivate children to try harder and they make obedience more appealing. As a result, the wise teacher or parent will select rewards that appeal specifically to the age level of the child. It's also wise to be familiar with the popular trends of the time.

I started teaching at the height of the Pac-Man™ craze, so every Friday my excellently behaved students were part of the "Perfect Pac-Man Club." My students loved it! They received a Perfect Pac-Man card on a bright rectangular piece of construction paper (about the size of a credit card). It said, "Perfect Pac-Man Club" and had the Pac-Man™ emblem on the front of the card. On the back was a scratch-and-sniff sticker with a quick note like, "Super Sara," "Terrific Tommy," or "Excellent Elizabeth." Since the cards were given out in a different random color from one time to the next, my students started collecting them at home. Some of my outstanding students would boast of how many they had collected.

Rewards should always be given in public. This honors the child receiving it and also inspires the other children to try to get into the limelight the next time by earning a reward. Always spell out exactly what the child has done to receive the reward.

Let's look at specific rewards for the classroom and the home.

Classroom Rewards

Classroom rewards can be given to individuals, small-groups, or the whole class, and are used to encourage the desired behavior in the students. All rewards work on the principle of bestowing special recognition to those students who "shine."

Individual Rewards

Individual rewards can include making a child the line leader or the teacher's helper, or any other type of noticeable activity that gives the child special recognition. Simple individual rewards could include extra recess, free time, a sticker, teacher's helper jobs such as picking up scraps while the other students are finishing an art project, erasing the chalkboard, taking down a bulletin board, taking a note to the office, handing out papers and supplies, or putting mail in the children's mailboxes.

In my classroom, I had a stuffed animal named *Percy*. Every morning he sat on my desk and watched all the kids doing their work. At various times throughout the morning, when it was quiet, I would say, "Oh, Percy is going to have such a tough time trying to choose someone today. There are so many good workers." After lunch, Percy told me who had been a quiet worker all morning. He gave specific examples of the child's outstanding behavior. Then he sat on that child's desk for the rest of the afternoon. *Percy was so loved by my students that even former students came back to visit my room and talk to him.*

Another useful reward I used at my weekly Bible Club—which could also be used when teaching Sunday School—was naming two children "Best Boy" and "Best Girl." This honor was saved until the end of the day and was bestowed on one outstanding boy and one girl. They received a small prize, like a balloon or a sticker or gum.

One little boy, Roberto, a nine-year-old in second grade, had completely frustrated his teachers in school. They had told his mother he was too difficult to stay in regular school. They wanted to send him to a school for children with extreme behavior disorders. But he showed a more teachable side in Bible Club. He was so eager to be named "Best Boy" that some days he would come to our Bible Club with a big grin and announce, "Roberto be 'Best Boy' today." He proceeded to obey perfectly all afternoon. When he was finally named "Best Boy," he beamed from ear to ear.

Don't inundate the students with too many rewards or they will lose their significance. For example, use either Percy or the "Best Boy and "Best Girl" awards, but don't use both at the same time.

Small-Group Rewards

A small-group reward is given to a group of students. The class can be divided by rows or by gender, or by whatever works. A group can be rewarded with being the first to go to recess, or they may all get a sticker. This type of competition encourages teamwork. The advantage to this type of reward is that children who might not care about pleasing the teacher, or care about the reward, will obey in order to please their peers.

Every week I kept a running tab of all the points each row earned for good behavior. This included being the first row to complete an assignment, or the first to get out their books and be ready for a new subject, or the first to clean up after an art project. By the end of the week, any row with at least 20 points received fresh popcorn. Every Friday afternoon before dismissal I would pop popcorn and dismiss each child from a winning row with a warm handful of popcorn. We had a rule that they had to wait to eat it until they were out of the building—this kept the floors clean. They looked forward to Fridays with great anticipation.

For some reason, many parents and students equated my name with *popcorn*. Later when I got married, I received four popcorn poppers!

Whole-Class Rewards

A whole-class reward requires the entire class to work as a team. They can receive points, or beans in a jar, or some other appropriate "counting" object. Once the goal amount of points or beans is achieved, the entire class receives the prize. Prizes can include such things as a special video, or ten extra minutes of recess.

The more creative the reward, the more the students will want to earn it. Throughout the day, continue to remind the children that they're doing a great job and that it will be hard to choose the "Best Boy" and "Best Girl," or whatever reward you have chosen to give.

Engineered Classroom

The "Engineered Classroom" is a very useful behavior system that I learned in graduate school. This system allows a teacher to keep track of a child's behavior one week at a time. Every Monday morning, I taped a 2-by 3-inch rectangle of construction paper to the top corner of each child's desk. It was labeled for the five days of the week. There was ample space on the card to record a child's good and bad behavior after the end of each day. I used a red and a green felt pen. For good behavior, a child received a green plus (+). Throughout the day, whenever I noticed good behavior, I walked over and put a green plus on the child's card. The student knew that at least five pluses per day for a week would result in a Perfect Pac-Man card on Friday. This was all the motivation a child needed.

The red pen was for bad behavior, like speaking out of turn or not working when everyone else was. One red minus (-) was considered a warning and the second meant that the child sat on the bench for five minutes during recess. If a child received more than two minuses in a week, that child could not be in the Perfect Pac-Man Club.

The nicest feature of this system was the fact that I could walk around the classroom with my two pens clipped on the belt of my dress or in my pocket so I had ready access to them. If a child came in from recess, sat down, and began doing his or her work, I quietly walked to the child's desk and marked the card with a green plus. We often exchanged smiles. I quietly walked around the desks acknowledging children who came in and got right to work.

Meanwhile, a child who came in and started talking or goofing off would freeze in dread at the sight of me walking toward his desk. "Oh no, here she comes with that red pen!" Without saying a word, I would put a minus on the child's card. We both knew he had just received the first warning. Another nice feature was that most of the child's anger or frustration was usually aimed at my red pen and not at me. Those pens stayed with me at all times and prevented me from nagging my students.

71

Home Rewards

At home, the types of rewards are numerous. Often, just genuine words of praise for a job well done will be reward enough. A child usually prefers the gift of time spent with the parent, sharing a fun—but not necessarily expensive—activity together, over getting another toy. What an honor it is to have the child value the relationship with the parent so highly!

The types of rewards used at home can be privileges, items, or outings. Below is a list of ideas to start you thinking of what you can use in your own home. The possibilities are endless. Have fun thinking up some of your own.

Privileges	Items	Outings
Read an extra story.	Ice cream cone.	Play at the park.
Have a friend over.	Special dessert.	Go to the beach.
Stay up 15 minutes later.	Inexpensive toy.	Fly kites.
Skip naptime.	Sticker.	Build sand castles.
Run through sprinklers	New art supplies,	Have a picnic.
Splash and play in rain.	such as small book,	Go to the zoo.
Play hide and seek.	crayons, scissors,etc.	Go to lunch or
Play game of child's	Candy.	dinner.
choice.	Money (pennies	Play in snow.
Extra TV or video time.	or nickels*)	See a movie.

* My sons get a penny for each weed they uproot, or snail they kill on their own time.

In a large family, it's nice to have a special outing with each child and the parent individually from time to time. This makes the child feel special and enhances the relationship with the parent.

Some of the bigger rewards, like the outings, may be earned over a period of days. A chart listing the days of the week, with rows for each area of obedience, can be very useful. The areas may include brushing teeth, washing hands, making the bed, feeding the dog, picking up toys, having a good attitude, or whatever daily routines you choose. If the child doesn't read yet, cut out pictures from magazines or draw simple figures that show what the areas are—a bed, a toothbrush, a dog, or a smiling face.

Once the child earns 15 or 20 stars or points—I let my boys put the stars on the chart as they earn them, they have earned a special outing or a special toy. I have a friend who still has fond memories of the Cinderella watch she earned with such a chart. Your child can take great pride in developing new skills and earning big rewards.

Task	Sun	Mon	Tue	Wed	Thu	Fri	Sat
Get Dressed	•	•	•	•	•	•	•
Make Bed		*			*		*
Brush Teeth	#	#	#	#	#	#	#
Feed Dog	†	†	†	†	†	†	†
Good Attitude	!	!	!	!	!	!	!

As a child develops the habit of making the bed, that item on the chart may be phased out and a new item put in its place. As your child gets older, the chart may lose its appeal. Be sensitive. If the child starts to lose interest, drop it. Once the interest wanes, the chart will be ineffective anyway.

Speaking of waning interests, if the ages between your children are great, you may want to individualize the rewards to match their interests. However, make sure the rewards are of equal worth. If one child gets an ice cream cone while another gets a day at the zoo for obeying the same rule, that's obviously unfair.

Dangers and Pitfalls

Parents and teachers must avoid two pitfalls when using rewards. As mentioned earlier, rewards for learning a new skill should be phased out gradually as the child develops the new skill. Also, every time a child is asked to do something basic, like sitting down for dinner, the result should not be a demand for a reward. Simple obedience is a part of life and when the child starts demanding a reward, the child has overstepped the boundaries. Not everything in life comes with a built-in reward. A child should be told that simple obedience is expected of him or her because the child is a part of the family.

The second pitfall comes with inadvertently rewarding bad behavior. At the grocery store, for instance, a child may know that if she screams, pleads, and throws a fit, her mom—out of sheer embarrassment—will eventually give in and buy her whatever she wants. The mother usually doesn't realize that she's being manipulated and has just rewarded the child for throwing a fit. Any time a parent or teacher gives a reward to a child as a means of stopping bad behavior, they are being manipulated by the child. They are encouraging the bad behavior to continue through the improper use of a reward.

A misbehaving child must be removed from everyone else and allowed to rejoin the family, or the activity, only after becoming quiet. This way, the child is not rewarded for the tantrum—rather, when the tantrum stops, the punishment for the tantrum ceases.

8
Levels of Offense

As you apply the principles and establish the preventions, sooner or later the inevitable will happen—a child will violate a rule and you must deliver a punishment. But first, you must determine the level of offense.

I've always found it a waste of time to ask children why they disobeyed. Too often, they shrug their shoulders and say, "I don't know," and most of the time, they speak the truth. Most children really don't know why they disobey. But there are always a few who knowingly tried to deceive me. Jeremiah 17:9 says, "The heart is more deceitful than all else and is desperately sick; who can understand it?" Therefore, it's your job as the parent or teacher to discern the intentions of the heart. What was the child's motive when disobeying?

The five levels of offense—in order from the least serious to the most serious—are *ignorance, forgetfulness, testing, rebellion*, and *danger*.

Ignorance

The first level of offense is *ignorance*—the child simply does not know the rule. Even though the teacher

77

or parent may have been careful to warn the child about a rule, there's always the chance the child was not paying attention, was out of the room, or was daydreaming at the time. The child may not know that a rule was broken.

The action to take is to state the rule and the consequence. Have the child repeat it back (just to guarantee that the child has heard). No punishment is given this time, but the child is reminded that next time there will be consequences.

Forgetfulness

The next level, *forgetfulness*, is similar to the first level. The difference is that you have already clearly stated the rule and you know the child has heard the rule. Young children may forget a new rule that they have not heard much, but you'll need to judge the situation. One or two warnings is more than enough for a kindergartner or first grader at the start of the year. As children grow older or familiar with a rule, they need only one warning.

Always ask yourself, "Did the child genuinely forget, or is the child just pretending to have forgotten?" If you feel the child genuinely forgot, and the rule is one that has been relayed only once or twice, then treat the situation the same way you treat ignorance. But if you think the child is pretending to forget, or the child is older, treat it as if the child is testing you.

The one-warning rule applies to all children, especially to those seven years or older. This doesn't mean that a child receives one warning per day. *He receives one warning and no more.* From that point he must be responsible for remembering the rule by himself. An adult may choose, however, to remind a forgetful child about a rule before the child enters a potentially hazardous setting where he may break the rule—like the grocery store. Giving extra warnings like this should be done with discretion since they may erode into nagging, which will be counterproductive.

Testing

Testing is when a child attempts to break the rules. This can be illustrated by a child who takes a cookie from the cookie jar knowing he or she should not. The child will go into the kitchen when the coast is clear and will quietly remove the cookie from the jar. Eating it quickly, the child will then try to clean up any crumbs or clues that might give the deed away, especially if the child is older and more sophisticated.

The child clearly knows the rule, but tries to step over the line anyway, and hopes not to be caught. This level of offense is characterized by guilt and caution. Even at a year old, my second son would stop and look cautiously over his shoulder right at me before he reached out to touch the knobs on the stereo. He never looked over his shoulder when he was doing what he knew to be right. At this young age, he was already showing me that he remembered the rules and was testing me to see how I would respond. Well, I did not disappoint him. I wanted to show him consistency and teach him that rules have consequences. Any child who is testing must receive the appropriate punishment immediately.

Rebellion

Rebellion, the next level of offense, is open defiance of the adult. The child who rebels is different from the testing child. The rebellious child will openly take a cookie while the adult is watching, and will look the adult in the eye with an open challenge, "I took this cookie and I'm eating it, so what are you going to do about it?" The rebellious child has a totally different attitude as he or she challenges the adult to see who is in control. This child needs to find out very fast just who is in control and must quickly suffer the consequences of wrong actions. The rebellious child must receive the standard punishment for the offense and may get a double dose.

Whenever a child rebels, he or she must be punished by the adult who was challenged. As a teacher, I rarely sent my students to the principal. I preferred to administer the punishment myself. In the same way, moms should not say, "Wait until your father gets home." Whenever a child challenges an adult's authority, the child wants to see who is in control the child or the adult. The child must find out quickly and beyond any doubt that it's the adult who is in control. Otherwise, the adult's authority is undermined and becomes weaker and weaker with every challenge the child wins. Ultimately, the child, even though continuing to win, will become unhappy and insecure, because the child knows that power and authority stop with him or her. A child really *needs* an adult who is older and wiser to be in that position. When the adult passes the child off to someone else for punishment, the adult has failed to meet the challenge and hopes someone else will be able to deal with the child.

The battle lines have been drawn, and the child boldly issues a challenge. Will a white flag of surrender fly in the breeze, or will the adult bravely meet the challenge with a determination to win.

A boy named Steven was the most rebellious student I had ever taught. In his short academic career, he had already been kicked out of four schools before he landed in my third grade class. This "con artist" began challenging me during the first few minutes on the first day of school. Within the next half hour, he used every trick he could think of to challenge my authority. As a result, he had worked himself into isolation and out the door to the principal. He made my head spin.

Prayer became my first weapon. I knew I needed extra wisdom in dealing with this child. During the first month of school he spent more time in isolation that he did sitting with the class. I knew we were at a stalemate and I didn't like it. I prayed again, asking for wisdom. God gave me the perfect solution.

One morning, I walked over to his desk, bent down, and very quietly but firmly started talking to him, man to man. Very seriously I told him, "Third grade is a fun place where the kids are excited about learning. But they can't have any fun until they learn to live by the rules. You're not living by the rules right now, but I wish you would, so you could join us and have some fun, too. I want you to like third grade and to think it was your best year. But right now you aren't living by the rules, and as long as you choose to break the rules in here, I'm going to do everything I can to make your life miserable. The choice is yours." A teacher had never spoken like this to him before, so he sat there in silence.

About an hour later, while the class was working quietly, I heard a faint *thud, thud, thud.* He was quietly thumping his head on his desk, not out of rebellion or to get attention, but as a sign of his final surrender. From that point on, he chose to abide by our class rules—most of the time anyway. He also enjoyed the rest of the school year.

I have a brave friend with a strong-willed six-year-old daughter. One morning before school the girl refused to get dressed by herself, even though she knew how. Her mother gave her plenty of warning, but the girl still refused to dress. Finally the mother said they would be leaving soon, and if she wasn't dressed she would go to school in her pajamas. She told her it would be unfair to make her brother late because of her willfulness. When it was time to leave, the girl still wore her pajamas. So the mother drove her to school that way. Once the final bell had rung and all of the children were in their rooms, she carried her defiant daughter in her pink, fuzzy-footed, pajamas to the office. The nurse and school secretary struggled to keep straight faces as the mother asked to use the nurse's room as a changing room.

The girl still insisted that she couldn't get dressed even though she had mastered this skill long ago. The mother reminded her that she could do this all by herself. Then she added that if she hurried, she would still make it to class in time for the opening. One last time, she waited to see if her mother was really serious. The mother didn't budge. Her daughter slowly began dressing. When she was nearly done, the mother helped her with her hair, and she hurried off to class.

The nurse and school secretary smiled, shook their heads, told the mother of their own strong-willed daughters, and said she had done the right thing. Their daughters were teens now and much harder to manage.

They told my friend that she was wise to win this battle while her daughter was only six.

The next day, the mother was again prepared for battle. She woke her daughter, and told her how much time she had to get ready. She reminded her that she could get dressed all by herself. Now she had a choice, did she want to dress at home or at school. She managed to dress before they left.

On the third day, she not only dressed herself, she even fixed her hair by herself. Then the mother started to reward her by allowing her to watch a little TV while she ate breakfast after she finished dressing. Suddenly the girl was eager to dress quickly.

A brave mother decided to confront her strong-willed daughter head on. The battle was difficult, but the mother refused to give in. Now her children dress themselves each morning, and she's free to save her energy to fight more important problems.

Danger

The last level of offense is *danger*. This is when a child threatens his or her own safety or the safety of others. It must be dealt with seriously. Often this may be very innocent, and the child may have no idea he or she is doing something that is potentially hazardous. It's wise to evaluate the intent of the child but, regardless of the intent, it must be stopped and punished immediately.

When our first son was just learning to walk, we told him to stay out of the street. If he darted into the street, he was quickly snatched up, appropriately punished *once*, and told, "No!" We had only one or two instances like this before he was cured of stepping into the street. In contrast, I know a mother who lies awake at night worrying about her son who frequently runs out into the street or into busy parking lots while she's trying to unload her other children from the car. She could easily cure her son—and catch up on her sleep—by punishing him each time until he learns. The small hurt of an appropriate punishment now is such a simple way to prevent a child from a big hurt later in life, such as permanent harm or even death.

Every year at school, I had at least one student who decided to play "Junior Scientist." The child would sit at his desk conducting experiments with books, paper, pens, and pencils. Eventually, he discovered that if he balanced his pencil halfway over the edge of his desk, he could smack his finger down on the extended side, and send the "pencil-missile" hurling across the room. During quiet work time, a few students might notice it, but most did not even know a pencil just flew over their heads while they were working. I intervened immediately to guarantee that the pencil's maiden voyage was its only voyage.

After calling the "scientist" to my desk and quietly discussing all the dangers and future punishments for such an offense, I confiscated the pencil for the day. If anyone had been hit, the child would have been punished, by the loss of recess and a written note of apology to the injured student. Then I told the class that all pens and pencils were to stay on their desks. If they were used for any other purpose, such as throwing or poking, the pencils became mine and the owner lost recess.

If the dangerous act committed was severe enough, then I punished a child even if the child had not been warned in advance.

A potentially dangerous situation may be when a child loses emotional control, or is on the verge of losing control. If in doing so he could threaten the safety of himself or others, then he should be restrained. In a group setting, a teacher must be quick to ensure the safety of all children in her care. At times this may require immediate action from the teacher—such as stopping a fight before it's started or a child has been injured.

One day when I taught Bible Club in East Palo Alto, I literally had to fly into action to prevent a major riot from occurring. Our Bible Club children were racially mixed, and growing up in the ghetto had heightened their racial tension. Without any warning, one of the boys started shouting angry racial slurs. I knew that the other children would take his insults personally, and a major riot could erupt.

I was leading songs at the time. I immediately stopped and went over to where he was. I had my partner take the children outside for an early game time. While I wrapped my arms tightly and firmly around this big nine-year-old so that his arms were held down to his sides, I waited for the room to empty. Softly but firmly I spoke to him in an effort to soothe his anger. I told him I would keep holding him until he calmed down and stopped fighting me. Then he starting hurling verbal anger at me and telling me how much he hated the "other race." Next he told me how much he hated me and how much he hated God. All the while he struggled and fought to get loose. I responded to his anger by telling him that I loved him and God loved him, too.

At one point he got loose and I had to chase him. Eventually he stopped fighting. I have no idea how much time passed until he finally stopped resisting and relaxed. I asked him if he was going to run away or shout any more racial slurs. He sighed and said, "No."

Physical restraint is not easy and it's no fun either, but it's far better than allowing a child to vent his anger on himself or others. Restraint should never be seen as a type of punishment, and the adult should never have the motive of using it to teach the child a lesson. It has only one purpose: *child safety*.

In the three years that I taught weekly Bible Clubs in East Palo Alto, I only had to use it once. It should be used only when *absolutely* necessary.

The following chart summarizes the five levels of offense. As the offense becomes more serious, the corresponding punishment must also be more severe.

Levels of Offense		
Level	**Definition**	**Action**
Ignorance	Child does not know the rule.	Clearly state rule; give a warning; no punishment
Forgetfulness	Child forgets the rule (especially true for young children).	Clearly state rule; give a warning; no punishment
Testing	Child tests boundaries by breaking a rule.	Administer punishment.
Rebellion	Child openly defies adult.	Administer strict punishment from same adult; double the punishment if necessary
Danger	Child threatens safety of self or others.	Administer immediate, strict punishment; no warning necessary

Main Obstacles to Obedience

Before leaving the five levels of offense, it's important to remember that sometimes when a child doesn't obey, it may have little to do with disobedience. The child may have been asked to do something he simply cannot do. Three main obstacles to obedience are: *mastery of a skill, development level,* and *emotional overload.*

Mastery of a skill

The mastery of a skill is a crucial part of the learning process. In education, when a child is learning a new skill—like counting to 20, the child may one day haltingly count all the way to 20. But the child has not mastered the skill until the child can confidently count to 20 without any errors or hesitation. Until the child reaches this point, the skill has not been mastered. During this time of intense learning, the most effective way to teach a child is with lots of praise, encouragement, and patience. If a parent or teacher is harsh and impatient, or punishes the child for not learning fast enough, the whole process will be undermined.

It's unfair to place the slow acquisition of a new skill in the same category as disobedience. Just because a child dressed himself or herself for the first time yesterday does not mean the child will have all of the confidence to dress without assistance today—especially if there are unfamiliar buttons, belts, snaps, zippers, or buckles. It may be awhile before the child feels confident enough to tackle the entire task alone. The child needs lots of encouragement during the process.

Punishment for failing to get dressed should only come after the child has consistently demonstrated mastery at dressing. Even then, I prefer to treat getting dressed as a game where the children compete with each other to see who can get dressed first. They have great fun and I'm there to assist the littlest child with any difficult parts.

Developmental level

So much of discipline depends on the child's age and abilities. If there is any doubt about whether or not a child can do something, then it should not be a discipline issue.

It's also wise to understand a child's level of intellect and comprehension. When communicating with a three-year-old, be sure to speak in terms a three-year-old can understand. Don't talk down to him, just use three-year-old language to explain new concepts. Try to get inside him and view life as a three-year-old.

A child is only capable of concrete reasoning before the age of eight. To me, one of the joys of teaching third-graders was having the privilege of introducing them to the world of abstract reasoning. But the child who thinks concretely, needs an adult to use concrete terms to communicate abstract truth.

When my son was four, he had intense fear of our huge dog. Nothing we tried diminished these fears. One day I decided to talk to him about fear, which is an abstract concept, as if it were a concrete object. I held my hands out as if I were holding an invisible basketball. I told him that his fear was as big as this. Then I told him if he would bravely face his fear of the dog, each time the fear would grow smaller and smaller. As I said this, I moved

88

my hands to show the invisible ball shrinking. Suddenly fear was a tangible object, and he felt he could deal with it.

An overriding theme in effective discipline must be setting reasonable expectations and rules for children.

I had taught third-graders for several years. One week I substituted in the first grade. The first two days I was frustrated with the students and their lack of maturity. Then one evening as I left for home, the light dawned. I expected first-graders to have the same attention span as third-graders. That was unrealistic. The next day, after I had adjusted my expectations, we had a great time learning together.

Emotional overload

A child's degree of fear may be so strong in a given setting that the child will be emotionally paralyzed, and may not be able to listen to the parent's commands, much less follow through with any action. At the age of two, my bold little son used to boss our huge Labrador around. Then one day, he suddenly became mortally afraid of the dog. This fear grew to include all dogs of all sizes. We tried not to overreact or encourage his fear. If he and the dog were both in the yard together, expecting simple obedience from my son was not so simple. He was paralyzed with fear. When either he or the dog was removed from the setting, however, he could be rational and act in obedience.

Parents should know their child better than anyone else. At the start of this chapter, both parents and teachers were reminded that it's their job to discern the intentions of the heart. A child should receive tolerance when undergoing some major trauma, like the death of a grandparent or a beloved pet. A child's parents may have just separated or maybe a friend has moved away. Whatever the situation, maybe the child is sick or missed a nap, parents should express understanding and give the child a little slack. However, this should never be confused with a license to disobey.

Removing a child from a potentially volatile situation is very different from excusing disobedience. For example, if a child who missed a nap is tired and whining, put the child to bed as soon as possible, before the child begins a battle with another sibling. Once the over-tired child has hurt a sibling, the parent may be very understanding of the situation, but the child still needs to see that wrong actions bring punishment. Claiming, "I didn't do it!" or "It was an accident!" should not absolve a guilty child of punishment.

One reason our nation's crime rate is rising so rapidly is that criminals have learned to blame everyone else for the crimes they commit. They say, "If only my parents had raised me differently. If only I could get a job. If only the government would help me out more. If only, if only . . ." Sooner or later we all need to take responsibility for our own actions. In the context of a loving home or classroom environment, we should help the children in our care to do their best even in adverse circumstances.

9
Penalties

Penalties are the exact opposite of rewards. Just as rewards are used to encourage good behavior, so penalties are used to punish bad behavior. Rewards should encourage good behavior by making it look appealing, while penalties should discourage bad behavior by making it look loathsome. Rewards should be presented in public so the child can feel honor for his worthy deeds. Penalties should be given privately so that the child is not embarrassed while others gaze on his disgrace.

This chapter will address the types of penalties, while the next chapter will describe how to administer punishment.

Once a child has broken a classroom or home rule, there are several kinds of penalties that may be used. These fall into four categories: loss of privilege, time out, natural consequences, and a trip to the principal. Penalties should be administered gradually. Some children will only need a mild rebuke.

Loss of Privileges

Loss of privileges is the first type of penalty. Often, I have watched children at a picnic trying to work their way through a plateful of food. Eventually, they run up to their mother and ask if they can play even though there is still a bunch of food on their plate. Inevitably, the mother surveys the plate. Ignoring the chips and cookie, she points out a half-eaten hot dog and says, "Just eat the meat. Then you can play." She knows what is crucial for good nutrition and what is not.

In the same way, an adult must determine which privileges are the "meat and vegetables" in a child's daily routine and which are "junk foods." Anything that qualifies as "junk food," is negotiable and can become a lost privilege. Meat and vegetables, however, are *never* negotiable.

Privileges should be lost for irresponsible or childish behavior. In the classroom, such lost privileges could be five minutes off recess, no art, no games, or no treat—an additional five minutes could be lost from recess for a second offense. Don't take them all away at once. One privilege should be taken away with each offense. Try to take away the privilege that will come next in the daily routine. This allows the child to quickly get his punishment "over with."

At home, lost privileges could be no dessert, removal of a toy that is not being used properly, no outing, no video, or no special activity. With older children, lost privileges could include loss of telephone time, an earlier bedtime, not going to a friend's house, or loss of allowance.

Except for cases of rebellion or danger, a child should be warned once about losing these privileges before they are gone.

The nice thing about lost privileges is that they can be used with one child or an entire group. I preferred not to punish the whole class, however, if I could find at least one or two children obeying, since it would have been unfair to punish them with the others.

Always remove one privilege at a time and warn the child of the consequences for the next offense. With each repeated or more serious offense, the penalty should become more severe. Be sure the privileges you choose to remove are ones you are willing to remove. Never threaten a child with taking away a privilege unless you intend to back it up with decisive action.

Types of behavior that might result in the loss of privilege at school are speaking out of turn, disrupting other kids who are trying to work, failure to do work, or any general minor disobedience.

The types of offenses at home that might result in the loss of a privilege are failure to eat a meal, the wrong use of a toy that could break it or damage other things, destructive behavior that is done with innocent motives, failure to complete a chore, or minor acts of disobedience.

With a child who is just learning to move about freely, the first battleground will probably be establishing "child-proof" boundaries. Touching dangerous items like lamp cords or delicate items like stereo knobs can be punished by first saying "No!" to the child as he crawls toward it. Then the second he reaches for it, the parent should pick him up, hold him to eye-level and say, "No touching, no touching!" Thus the process of understanding for the child starts. Then the parent should place the child far away facing a different direction. He has just lost the privilege of touching anything he chooses.

Only very compliant children will quit after a first rebuke. Most children will test boundaries again and again. Be prepared to enforce those danger zones every time. Eventually the child will lose interest and find something else to explore.

Isolation or Time Out

Isolation or time out is reserved for repeated offenses. Isolation or time out is the ultimate loss of privilege. The purpose of time out is to correct a bad attitude that has led to the repeated offenses. The child stays in *time out* until the attitude is adjusted.

When I gave a child isolation in the classroom, she would have to move her desk to a far corner. She spoke to no one and no one spoke to her. She was told to quietly do her work. Once she demonstrated a good, consistent attitude, she was able to return to her normal place. Since a child's attitude determines how long she must be in isolation, most children remain in isolation for only one to two hours. Occasionally, a rare child with a stubborn attitude would remain in isolation one or two days. Once her attitude was adjusted and she chose to live by the classroom rules, which was usually demonstrated by the completion of assignments that had been neglected as a result of bad behavior, she would rejoin the class. In my classroom, every child knew that isolation was the last stop. If behavior got worse, a trip to the principal was next.

At home, time out can be spent on a chair in the corner or in an unused room. The duration should be in relation to the child's age as well as his attitude. When our son was 15 months old and he screamed angrily, I would tell him that when he was quiet, I would come and get him out of the playpen, which had been put in another room. When there was a lull in the screaming, I quickly picked him up and said, "My, it's so quiet!" He learned to get quiet sooner and sooner, until the screaming stopped altogether. Whenever our three-year-old expressed a bad attitude or started to tantrum, I would give him a time out and set the timer for three minutes. When it rang, I would talk to him about why he had time out, and I would let him go if he had a good attitude.

Natural Consequences

Wrong actions often create their own built-in consequences. A wise adult will look for opportunities to allow children to learn from their own wrong actions. If a child makes a terrible mess in her room, she must clean up the mess. She is responsible for her own actions. If a child breaks a sibling's toy, not only must she apologize but she must buy a new toy with her own money to replace it. If a child breaks an expensive item in the home—especially if there is malicious intent, she needs to be given a reasonable amount of work that is appropriate for her age level. This allows her to earn the necessary amount to cover the cost of replacing the item.

The same principles apply at school if a child damages school property or another student's property. All concerned parents and teachers should reach an agreeable solution that includes the type and amount of work required to fix or replace the damaged object.

When a child in the classroom leaned back on his chair, there was always the risk that he would fall and smack the back of his head on the floor. As a result, whenever a child started to lean back on his chair I warned him that if he leaned back again, I would take his chair away and he would have to *kneel* at his desk in order to do his work until the next recess. The mere threat of this punishment was quite effective. I rarely had to take away anyone's chair.

Being Sent to the Principal or Suspension

For repeated, willful disobedience or rebellion at school, a child is sent to the principal. This is reserved for the stubborn or rebellious child who has not responded to the milder types of penalties. I chose to deal with as many discipline problems with my students as possible. If a child was in isolation and still refused to obey, he was sent to the principal.

In a Sunday School or Vacation Bible School setting where there is no principal, suspension is the ultimate penalty. The child who is willfully disobedient, or is threatening the safety of other children has lost the privilege of staying with the group. Just as many churches have a silent pager for parents with fussy babies in the nursery, so parents should be paged to remove a child who is biting or scratching other children. Sunday School should be a safe place for all children. One angry child shouldn't be allowed to spoil it for the others.

Long Term Results

I want my children to grow in favor with God and with man just as Jesus did. If I work off their rough edges at home in a loving environment, then God will be able to use them more fully, and they will find favor with their teachers and classmates. The big world will be a lot less forgiving to my children than I am, so it's in their best interest to learn life's hard lessons at home.

Hebrews 12:7-11 says:

Endure hardship as discipline; God is treating you as sons. For what son is not disciplined by his father? If you are not disciplined (and everyone undergoes discipline), then you are illegitimate children and not true sons. Moreover, we have all had human fathers who disciplined us and we respected them for it. How much more should we submit to the Father of our spirits and live! Our fathers disciplined us for a little while as they thought best; but God disciplines us for our good, that we may share in his holiness. No discipline seems pleasant at the time, but painful. Later on, however, it produces a harvest of righteousness and peace for those who have been trained by it.

God's discipline is painful, but ultimately it produces a harvest of righteousness and peace, which is for our profit. As parents and teachers, this should also be the goal of our punishment as we seek the best for each child in our care.

10
Administering Punishment

Once the appropriate penalty has been chosen to fit the offense, you are ready to administer the punishment.

Because punishment administered carelessly or harshly has the potential of being destructive, there are guidelines to follow in making it constructive, so the child grows and develops better behavior as a result. The attitude of the parent or the teacher administering the punishment and the way the punishment is given will determine whether or not the child benefits from the punishment. Keep in mind that even the right punishment given in the wrong way can have negative consequences.

Anytime there is a conflict and the child needs punishment, two extreme responses can damage the relationship with the child. On one extreme, the adult who is harsh, angry, or vengeful will create a wall of resistance in the child being punished. If this continues over time, bitterness and hatred will grow toward the adult. On the other extreme, a parent or teacher who backs down or apologizes for punishing will lose respect in the eyes of the child. In the middle of these two extremes is a balanced approach that, if administered according to the steps below, will build a closer relationship with the child and will encourage better behavior in the future.

The eight steps to administering punishment are: *always punish in private; always be calm and firm; determine what happened; discern the level of offense; stress the specific offense; deliver the penalty; discuss future prevention;* and *never allow the child to blame you.*

1. Always punish in private.

This is in direct contrast to rewards, which are given in public. Never humiliate a child in front of others, even siblings. Remove the child from the group and, if possible, go to an inconspicuous place. If it's impossible to be completely out of the sight of others, at least speak quietly so others cannot hear. If a child is punished in front of others, he will be so concerned about what the others think, he will not be paying attention. He may also be more defensive as a result.

2. Always be calm and firm.

Use a soft tone of voice. Proverbs 15:1 says, "A gentle answer turns away wrath, but a harsh word stirs up anger." Since the child just disobeyed, you may be very angry. If this is the case, have him sit somewhere and wait until you feel cool enough to deal with him calmly. Establishing the right tone is crucial to effective discipline. It impacts how the child receives it. Otherwise, a volatile clash may erupt instead of a meeting of the hearts. Even though your voice is soft, your manner should be firm and matter of fact, not vindictive.

Be sure to maintain eye contact. If the child cannot look at you, then tell him that you will wait until he does. Then you should wait silently. If the child is looking at the floor, ceiling, or anywhere else, your words will not get through. With my young sons there are times when they are defiantly looking anywhere else but at me. When that happens, I will firmly but gently hold their chin in my hand and turn their face until we are eye to eye. If necessary, throughout the procedure remind a child to look at you.

A gentle touch can reassure the child he is not being rejected. Get on the same level as the child; don't look down on him. Kneel or sit down to make sure you are at the child's eye-level. At school, I would always call a child up to my desk, put my arm around him , and quietly discuss the need for punishment. It was like a private conference. While sitting in my chair, I would be at eye-level with the child standing beside me. With my arm around him, I could often feel his rigid posture relax as he recognized through my touch that I wasn't angry with him and still accepted him, but was disappointed with his behavior.

3. Determine what happened.

Always ask a child what he did. Don't ask him why he did it. Most of the time a child doesn't know why. If you saw the incident, then this step is simple. But if you did not see it happen, you must do your best to get the full story. If multiple children were involved, listen to each one's story. At all times as the child is speaking, express caring and concern. Often the child disobeyed because his feelings were hurt or he may have been frustrated about something.

4. Discern the level of offense.

Was it ignorance, forgetfulness, testing, rebellion, or danger? This will help to determine the degree or type of punishment.

5. Discuss the specific offense.

The child should confess to committing the specific offense. You should ask him a direct question. "Did you kick Billy?"

The child should respond, "Yes, I did."

Then ask the child to tell you what the penalty for his wrong action will be. "Well, what happens when you kick Billy?" The child should respond with the penalty.

If the child will not admit that he committed the offense, but you know that he did, then tell him that he will be punished even though he doesn't confess. If he lies, tell him he will receive a double penalty for lying. Lying is very serious and must be treated as such.

6. Deliver the penalty.

Chapter nine presents a list of possible penalties. While delivering the penalty, your attitude must be matter of fact and somber. It cannot be stressed enough that if a child senses that you enjoy punishing him, the relationship will be seriously undermined.

7. Stress future prevention.

Ask the child, "How will you avoid this in the future?" Help the child find one or two good alternatives so he doesn't repeat the same offense. Often the child will find himself in a similar situation, same time, same place, tomorrow. So help him plan one or two alternative ways to handle the situation the next time it arises.

With a young child, carefully discuss one alternative plan, have him repeat it back to you so it is clear that he understood. This will also help him remember the plan.

8. Never allow the child to blame you.

The reason that the child has been punished should not be blamed on you. The child's disobedience was not your fault. The child must accept responsibility for his own actions. If he is angry at you, then he is heaping the blame on you. If the rules have been laid out and he has been warned of punishment, and he chooses to disobey, then he has chosen to be punished. All the responsibility for his actions must be placed firmly on his shoulders. He must see that he chose to break the rules, and he chose to suffer the consequences for his actions. If he becomes angry with you, then you should think back through the above steps and make sure that your attitude is what it should be. If your attitude hasn't been right, then you should apologize and correct your attitude first. Then the child's wrong action should be discussed and the child should recognize that he chose to disobey, and therefore chose to be punished. The child must not be allowed to return to his normal play or routine until he takes responsibility for his wrong actions.

Our state jails and prisons are filled with people who have never taken responsibility for their own actions. Children must learn to take responsibility for their own actions while they're still young. Proverbs 29:1 says, "He who hardens his neck after much reproof will be crushed beyond remedy." This verse aptly describes a hard, stubborn, or rebellious child who stiffens his neck and tries to heap the blame and guilt for his punishment on you. If this pattern continues, then one day he will be crushed beyond remedy, either through our justice system, or from the inevitable consequences of his rebellious, uncontrolled behavior.

If you spend too much time discussing the wrong action, especially before the punishment is given, the child who is hungry for attention may repeat the offense to get more. This is merely a reminder to always save the discussion of prevention until after the punishment has been given. This is also a reminder that if a child is not receiving plenty of positive attention from you, he may seek it through disobedience.

The best way to illustrate this system of administering punishment is with a story of one challenging boy in my class, and how I dealt with him.

It had been one of those days. I had a student named Billy who had constantly challenged me all morning. He had already lost his recess and his privileges. Things had escalated to the point where I needed to isolate him. He moved his desk and chair to a remote corner in the back of the classroom next to the counter and a sink. The rest of the students were quietly working at their desks when we heard the rushing sound of a waterfall. Immediately, half a dozen kids gasped and raised their hands to inform me of Billy's latest offense. He had filled his mouth with water from the drinking fountain and had sprayed it all over the linoleum. I calmly walked back to his desk, where he was suddenly very interested in his school work. I asked him to stand. We walked over to the large puddle on the floor and carefully surveyed the situation. I put my arm around his shoulders and asked him, "What is this?"

"Water," he replied.

"Do you know how it got there?" I asked.

"I put it there," he said and flashed me a sheepish grin.

At this point, I was so angry with him that I told him to sit at his desk and not move until I came back to talk to him. I walked to my desk thinking of James 1:5, which says, "If any of you lacks wisdom, he should ask God, who gives generously to all without finding fault, and it will be given to him." I quickly prayed for wisdom. I knew the punishment needed to fit the crime.

Now, water on linoleum did not cause any damage, but he was acting in rebellion. I had never made a specific rule about spitting on the floor, for it was understood by all that it wasn't to be done. I knew Billy needed to be punished and I wanted to make sure I chose an appropriate punishment.

Fortunately, the class was dismissed for choir, so I could be alone with Billy. Still praying for wisdom, I quietly walked back to his desk. Opening the cupboard beneath the sink, I produced a sponge and some cleanser. Very calmly but firmly I told him that spitting was not allowed in our classroom. Because he had spit on the floor, he now needed to clean the floor. I sprinkled some cleanser over the puddle and handed him the sponge.

He stood there in shock holding the sponge as I walked back to my desk. "You can't do this to me," he said.

"Oh yes, I can. If you spit on my floor, you clean my floor," I replied, and began working on some paperwork at my desk. Out of the corner of my eye I saw him standing there just watching me, hoping to call my bluff, but I wasn't bluffing.

Eventually, he dropped down to his knees and started scrubbing. A few minutes later, he timidly came to my desk and told me he was done. Together we went and inspected his work. I pointed out a black heel mark and some ground-in green crayon that needed to be removed.

A few minutes later, he returned and said he was done. Together we went and inspected his work again. This time the floor looked great, and I told him so. He

105

had done a good job. All of his anger and rebellion had been scrubbed away like the dirt on the floor.

"Can I go to choir now?" asked the boy who hated going to choir. As he walked out the door, there was a lilt in his step. He had paid for his crime and was a free man. I'm sure he won't spit on anyone's floor again.

Later, when I shared the incident with my principal, he was pleased with what I had done with Billy. But he told me the cleanser had stripped all the wax off the floor. OOPS!

The change in Billy's attitude from open rebellion, to a soft submissive spirit, to a carefree boy on his way to choir is the goal of effective discipline. When the penalty has been carefully selected and administered with the right attitude, a child's heart will be softened, and he will have the resolve to do better in the future. And there is no need to bring it up again, because he has paid his penalty.

11
Settling Disputes

There is an old saying, "When Momma ain't happy, ain't nobody happy." While I was coping with a three-week chicken pox quarantine, I recognized the wisdom in this saying. On days when I was calm, soothing, and sensitive to my children's needs our atmosphere was peaceful. But on days when I was stressed, preoccupied, and needed space, the children responded by whining, clinging, and bickering. On one such day, as I rushed out the door while they fussed with a babysitter, I realized that I was the emotional thermostat in my home.

In the classroom this principle is also true. On days when I was positive and gave the students my complete attention, they were eager to learn. But on days when I was preoccupied and insensitive to them, they lost the motivation to learn and often discord broke out. *The teacher is the emotional thermostat for the classroom.*

As the emotional thermostat, when an adult is calm and sensitive, fewer disputes should erupt. Nevertheless, because of human nature, some disputes will occur. When they occur, the adult needs to use the opportunity for developing better social skills. The skills siblings develop as they interact will be transferred to their peers. If siblings learn to resolve their differences peaceably, they will also be able resolve problems with peers. The home is the first place a child will learn to resolve conflict. The classroom is the second place.

Both parents and teachers play many roles in a day as they interact with their children. These roles may include being a nurse, secretary, counselor, maid, or judge. A full-time judge will not pronounce the verdict until after weighing all the evidence. So a wise parent or teacher will weigh all of the facts first.

When a dispute arises, there are five steps to take:

1. Collect all the children who were involved.

Since most disputes happen on the playground, it's likely that the teacher didn't see what happened. In order to get 100% of the story, the teacher must hear from every involved child. If the teacher was fortunate enough to see the incident this will be much easier, but it's still wise to hear from every child who was involved.

2. Listen to each child's account—listening especially for specific offenses.

Ask questions to get the full picture if something needs clarification. Be sure to get the sequence of events. Whenever a fight broke out, the boy who threw the first punch was considered the instigator and received a greater penalty. Therefore, a child who started the dispute should be seen as the instigator. Usually no one is completely innocent and each has contributed to the problem. In a preschool setting or with pre-language children, the adult needs to be careful to try and fill in the missing pieces of the story. Do not punish a child with only partial information.

3. Explain the specific offenses of each child and the consequences.

Each child needs to be punished for his or her wrong actions. Even though others may have been wrong, each child must accept responsibility for his own actions.

A teacher could respond by saying, "Child #1, you called child #2 a name. What is our punishment for name calling?"

Then the teacher could face child #2 and say, "Child #2, you punched child #1. What is our punishment for punching?" At this point, each child must face the consequences for his actions.

4. Stress apology and forgiveness.

The offender needs to apologize to the victim. The old saying, "Sticks and stones can break my bones, but names will never hurt me," is not always true. Often unkind words can cut into the heart of their victim. On a personal note, I still remember some very cruel things that were said to me in Jr. High. I remember the people and the exact words they used.

By third grade, a child can write a letter of apology and needs to end it by listing three qualities she likes or admires about the victim. This helps to build up the child who was emotionally wounded. The child must write this letter during recess time. I always checked it before it was delivered.

In our home, there are usually two guilty parties. Once each has apologized, they are eager to forgive. They hug and are buddies again. So far, my boys haven't struggled with forgiveness.

But during my teacher days, I had several students struggle with forgiveness. They were all girls. As a result,

I had to develop a strategy for working with my unforgiving students. I reminded each of the warning in Matthew 6:14-15 where Jesus says, "For if you forgive men when they sin against you, Your heavenly Father will also forgive you. But if you do not forgive men their sins, your Father will not forgive your sins." This gave the student a whole new reason to forgive. Once the process was complete, I had the kids hug or shake hands.

5. Stress kindness and empathy throughout the entire process.

There's a good chance that tomorrow, the same time, the same place, a similar problem could erupt between the same children. The more a child's sensitivity toward others is encouraged, the less he will act hurtfully. I wanted the children to monitor their own actions by asking themselves if a given action was kind or hurtful before the action had been committed. So I talked with the children about a kind option. One of the best preventions is to help children see how their actions hurt other children. I asked them, "How would you feel if this was done to you?" Then we discussed ways to avoid similar problems in the future.

My son's Christian school has the same poster mounted in every classroom. It simply says, "Do unto others as you would have them do unto you. There is no other rule." If everyone would live by this Golden Rule, there would be no wars or crime.

At home, when tensions mount and tempers flare between the boys and I haven't seen what happened, I follow the same five steps given above. But when I am dealing with one child who can speak and with one who is too young to speak, they both get time out. Under this condition, it would be unfair to hear only one story. When they can both communicate clearly, I use the above steps. Then I separate them and give them both time out until they cool down. When they're finally ready to play again, they hug each other and play together with a peaceful attitude.

The Passive-Aggressive Child

When two children are involved in repeated conflicts, and one child always seems to get in trouble, while the other child never seems to be at fault, look closely for all of the details. A passive-aggressive child is a master at manipulating others. She is often a quiet, thoughtful, clever, older child. She knows exactly what buttons to push in order to aggravate another into making trouble. Meanwhile the child who keeps getting in trouble doesn't even know he's being lured into another trap. If you notice this trend emerging, you would be wise to hesitate before punishing, and start investigating for more details. If the passive-aggressive child is tempting another to break the rules, she should share the punishment. After all, she was an accomplice.

Squabblers or Nitpickers

Inevitably, every year at school that magic combination of two children with neighboring desks will explode into full-fledged squabbling. It's usually a boy and a girl, with the usual complaints.

"His paper keeps getting onto my desk."

"She won't stop humming."

"He is bugging me."

"She keeps looking at me."

And on and on it goes.

When this happens, tell both children that they must focus on doing their own work and stop worrying about their neighbor. If this doesn't work and they continue to complain, then warn them of the ultimate punishment— isolation together. This is such a mortifying thought that most kids are willing to resolve their differences on the spot.

One mother with 10-and 12-year-olds told me she did the same thing with her children. Whenever they started to squabble, she sent them both to the same room and told them they had to work out their difficulties before they could come out. Then she shut the door. Once they resolved their problem, they told her their solution. In the process, they became effective problem solvers.

Favoritism

Favoritism creates a lot of trouble between siblings. It can also create problems between students. Every class of students will contain a few adorable children, a bunch of average children, and a few hard-to-love children. Teachers must do their best to treat all students equally regardless of personal feelings. This is important for the best interests of all concerned.

The adorable child who frequently gets more than her share of attention, may end up being spurned by peers who look on jealously. At recess she may be labeled, "teacher's pet," or worse. Meanwhile, the average students may grow to resent the teacher for rarely even recognizing them. The hard-to-love child may not have any friends, and the teacher's insensitivity toward him may create greater self-doubt and insecurity. If this continues for several years, it will encourage a negative response toward other authority figures, since he will perceive all in authority as unfair.

A wise teacher will see all children in her classroom as equals. She knows that no one wins when she plays favorites. She will do her best to spread around the honors and recognition as equally as possible. She will be sensitive to the underdogs in her classroom and seek to build them up. In the process, there will be less disputes to deal with.

12
Sibling Rivalry

Sibling rivalry has been with mankind since the beginning of time. The book of Genesis records four different cases of intense sibling rivalry. Three stories were between brothers and one was between sisters. All involved jealousy and favoritism. All the cases between the brothers were so intense that the elder brothers intended to kill the younger, favored, brother. The four cases of sibling rivalry were Cain and Abel, Jacob and Esau, Rachel and Leah, and Joseph and his brothers.

Siblings from Scripture

Cain and Abel were the first brothers born to mankind. Genesis 4:1-8 gives the account of how God accepted Abel's offering of the first born from his flock. God rejected Cain's offering of fruit. God expected offerings to be animal sacrifices, so only Abel's offering was acceptable. In Genesis 4:7, God told Cain, "If you do what is right, will you not be accepted? But if you do not do what is right sin is crouching at your door; it desires to have you, but you must master it." All Cain needed to do was to obey God by giving an animal sacrifice, which God would accept. But, instead, he chose to kill Abel.

Jacob and Esau were twins born to Isaac and Rebekah. Their story starts in Genesis 25:21-34. They struggled with each other before they were even born. The parents each chose a favorite son. Isaac chose Esau because he was a mighty hunter who brought back savory meat for his father. Rebekah chose Jacob because he was a quiet, peaceful man who preferred to work around the tents. From that point on, the family was split into these two teams. The competition was intense. First Jacob purchased Esau's birthright from him for bread and a pot of lentil stew.

After this, there was only one favor left that Isaac could give Esau: a blessing. Rebekah and Jacob schemed to take this also. The story unfolds in Genesis 27:1-45. Jacob dressed in Esau's clothes so he felt and smelled like Esau. This tricked blind Isaac into giving the blessing to Jacob. Once Jacob had the blessing, Esau planned to kill him. So Jacob literally fled for his life at Rebekah's recommendation. "Your brother Esau is consoling himself with the thought of killing you. Now then, my son, do what I say: Flee at once to my brother Laban in Haran" (Genesis 27:43-44).

Rachel and Leah were Laban's daughters. Their rivalry begins in Genesis 29:17-18, which says, "Leah had weak eyes, but Rachel was lovely in form and beautiful. Jacob was in love with Rachel." Then verse 30 says, ". . . he loved Rachel more than Leah."

Let's look at this story from Leah's perspective. No eligible bachelor had expressed interest in her, so her father was afraid she would end up a spinster. Then cousin Jacob came along and fell head over heels in love with her beautiful younger sister. He worked seven long years to earn the privilege of marrying Rachel. On the wedding night, the girls' father, Laban, had Leah pretend to be Rachel. The next morning, Jacob discovered that his new bride was Leah! How humiliating for Leah to live with Jacob's rejection. It wasn't bad enough to have a gorgeous sister—now the rest of her life she would have to share the same husband with Rachel.

As the two sisters competed for Jacob's love, Joseph and his brothers were born as a result of this rivalry. The ten older brothers were sons of Leah or two other concubines. At last Joseph was born to Rachel. All the sons were mere pawns in this game as their mothers sought to win the most favor with Jacob. The problems start for Joseph in Genesis 37:3-4 which records, "Now Israel loved Joseph more than any of his other sons, because he had been born to him in his old age; and he made a richly ornamented robe for him. When his brothers saw that their father loved him more than any of them, they hated him and could not speak a kind word to him."

The ten older brothers knew Joseph was Jacob's favorite, so they hated him. They couldn't get love from Jacob, so they hated Joseph because he had the one thing they couldn't get. Later, when Joseph was out in the fields with them, they plotted to kill him. After beating him, they threw him into a dry well. Eventually they sold him as a slave.

117

Sibling rivalry is also found in the story of David and his brothers, and the sons of David. In all these accounts, jealousy and favoritism fuel the fire of sibling rivalry.

Today, as we seek to raise our children, this issue of sibling rivalry must be faced, and we need to do what we can to prevent this natural tendency from escalating into open warfare.

It's wise to look at some of the themes that repeat themselves in the Scripture stories. Siblings of the same sex tend to compete more, the older child opposes the younger, and parental favoritism leads to resentment from the sibling. Parents today should learn from the mistakes of these ancient parents and minimize the rivalry in their homes.

Same Sex Siblings

The first similarity in all of these stories is that the rivalry was between siblings of the same sex. It may happen between children of opposite sexes, but the trend is between those of the same sex. Many mothers with one son and one daughter have said that sibling rivalry is very minor between their children. The son knows that his world consists of trucks and baseball, while the daughter's consists of dolls and ballet. Each feels secure that the other won't intrude on their space. Clearly, competition between two siblings of the same sex will be more intense. As a result, parents must find ways to minimize this.

Older versus Younger

In all of the Genesis accounts, the second theme is: *The older child is jealous of the younger child.* Cain hates Abel, the younger brother. Esau hates Jacob, the younger brother. Leah hates Rachel, the younger sister. The ten brothers hate Joseph, the younger brother. This truth is also revealed in research on family dynamics. A first child is accustomed to the parents' full attention. If a second sibling comes after he turns four and has a strong sense of self, he will be less threatened. But if the second child comes earlier, the younger he is the more threatened he will feel, since the baby is crowding his space with Mom and Dad. Thus, generally a two-year-old will tend to feel more threatened than a three-year-old.

It's interesting to note that when a third child joins the family, the sibling transition is usually smoother. This is because the second child has learned to share the parents with the older child. As a result, the new baby poses less of a threat.

When my fourth child was born, the pediatrician came to the hospital to check the baby and make sure she was healthy. He spent more talking to me about my 17-month-old than he did about my newborn. He reminded me that my son was still a baby and had strong emotional needs for me. He told me to be careful not to push him aside when I was caring for the newborn. This was a vulnerable time in his life.

This trend of favoring a younger child can be seen today as often "the baby" is pampered and given whatever he or she wants. In the four stories from Genesis, favoritism fueled the flame of rivalry into an inferno.

Favoritism from the Parent

Favoritism from the parent will usually grow into resentment from the "unfavored" sibling. That resentment can erupt into full-blown hatred.

A friend grew up as one of four daughters. Two

sisters received special favors, while two did not. My friend received the favors. As a child, she enjoyed this special treatment, but when she grew, she recognized her other two sisters received less. As a result, she felt sorry for them. One of the unfavored sisters has grown to resent my friend. Today as adults, the two favorites still receive special treatment. The resentment from the unfavored sister has grown strong over the years. In a family where favoritism is shown, no one wins.

In conclusion, the three themes from Genesis are: same sex siblings will compete more, the older child may resent the younger, and favoritism will intensify the problem.

If your first and second child are of the same sex and closely spaced, there is a strong chance the older will resent the younger. If there is any favoritism, the resentment will be magnified.

Minimizing Rivalry

The classic response of an older child when a new baby comes home from the hospital is to dump the baby out of the cradle. Since this is the natural response, let's look at seven steps to minimize this rivalry.

1. Prepare for the baby.

If possible, before the birth of the baby, begin preparing the older child who will feel threatened and misplaced. This can affect many different areas of the child's life. If the child is still sleeping in the crib, it would be wise to graduate her into a big bed. This may be merely a mattress on the floor until she's ready to sleep up high on a big bed without the crib bars to contain her. Make a big deal of it. Tell her she is now a BIG girl and doesn't need a little baby crib anymore. Do this a month or more before the baby is born. Put the crib in a closet out of sight, so the memory of it will fade. This gives the older child time to adjust to the new bed. Once the baby is done sleeping in the cradle, the crib is set up again.

At the birth of each new sibling, we kept a tradition of giving the older child a gift from the baby. I always wrapped an exciting toy and brought it home in my suitcase. When the big brothers arrived to meet their new baby, they were greeted with a great present. I told them the gift was from their new baby because he was so excited to have them for big brothers.

The gift has worked wonders in winning over the big brothers. When my third son, Caleb, was born, my oldest son, John, was determined to have baby Samson for his new brother. I told him that his new brother would be Caleb. John insisted that he would be Samson. When I called him with the news of baby Caleb's birth, there was silence on the other end of the line. He finally said, "Well, I guess we can take baby Caleb home, but when we get tired of him, we'll take him back to the hospital and trade him in for baby Samson." The next day when he arrived at the hospital, baby Caleb gave him a super gift. As he opened the gift, his eyes lit up and he exclaimed, "Wow! baby Caleb is a neat baby!" Because baby Caleb had great taste in gifts, that was the last we heard of "baby Samson."

It's also helpful to tell the child how much the baby wants to be like them. New babies require a lot of attention, so when the baby starts to nurse, I tell the older child how much the baby wants to be big and eat food like the big brother. When the baby needs a diaper change, I tell the older child how much the baby wants to wear big-boy pants like big brother. I look for opportunities to build up the older child and make the baby his #1 fan. This is true—younger siblings want to be like older siblings so let them wear their big brother status with pride.

We all shared ownership for the baby. If the baby started to cry while I was busy fixing dinner, I would tell one of the boys, "Our baby sounds sad. Could you sing her a song or find her a toy?" They gladly helped take care of *our* baby. Even today, when our oldest is at school, sometimes, the younger ones will say, "We miss our John at school." They have a strong sense of belonging to each other and are quick to help each other.

2. Eliminate favoritism.

Favoritism, or unequal treatment, can create major problems. In the stories from the Scriptures there were two types of favoritism: perceived and genuine.

Perceived favoritism is not real , but from the child's vantage point it sure looks like favoritism. Children have a myopic view of the world. They are like a horse with blinders; they can only see life from their narrow viewpoint. As an adult we have a much broader field of vision. We can see the big picture. If a child accuses us of being unfair when we know we were being fair, we must broaden our child's viewpoint.

One day my son complained that his younger brother had a friend come to play but he didn't get to have a friend over. So, I asked him, "Who played in a baseball game yesterday while the whole family cheered?"

"I did," he said.

"Who got to go to a birthday party last week?" I asked.

"I did," he replied.

"Did your brother get to play in a baseball game or go to a birthday party?" I asked

"No," he said.

"Well, then, who should get a turn to have a friend come over?" I asked once more.

"It's Gabriel's turn," he slowly replied.

Instead of getting angry with him, I merely broadened his vantage point so he could see the bigger picture. The more you do this with your child, the less selfish he will be in his thinking, and the more considerate of others.

In the story of Cain and Abel, Cain perceived that God was showing favoritism to Abel. God had told them to offer animal sacrifices, but Cain chose to offer fruit. Because Cain did not want to play by the rules, God could not accept his offering. In Genesis 4:7, God confronts Cain while he sulks, "If you do well, will not your countenance be lifted up? and if you do not do well, sin is crouching at the door; and its desire is for you, but you must master it." God told Cain if he would only follow the rules, he would be happy. He reminded Cain that he must make a choice: to follow his sin nature or master it. Unfortunately, Cain made the wrong choice and murdered his brother.

If our children make wrong choices and lose privileges that others have, they need to see that they are feeling the consequences of their own actions, and that it's not a reflection of the parent's feelings toward them. If the favoritism is real, however, it's more difficult to deal with.

Reasons for Favoritism

There are three root causes to favoritism: *birth order, unrealistic expectations,* and *reflection of the parent's flaws.*

a. Birth order.

Since the first child is the only child in the home for some time, he gets a lot of attention from Mom and Dad. They are free to monitor his actions closely. As each new child enters the family, however, the younger child receives less scrutiny and can often get away with more, since the parents are busy trying to juggle caring for all the needs of all the children. The oldest may say, "You didn't let me do that when I was their age." On top of this, the oldest is often needed to help care for the younger ones.

In our home, I struggle with this. Many times I do need the older child's help. I also know that I cannot monitor my little ones as closely as I monitored the older ones when they were small. But I try to minimize these distinctions. When an older child is responsible for doing certain jobs, I make sure he gets extra privileges. I also make sure he receives lots of praise for a job well done. As a result he is very proud of his big brother status.

b. Unrealistic expectations.

Before my first child was born, my friend, Jonnette, wisely said, "The Gerber baby is a myth invented by some ad agency." It is so easy for an expectant mother to have idealistic expectations about motherhood and about her new baby. Each mother's ideal baby will be different, most babies will not meet up to those expectations. If a mother longs for a brown-eyed son with dark curly hair, and gets a bald daughter, she may be disappointed. A child that comes at the wrong time, of the wrong sex, or with the wrong physical features may disappoint the parents. The sad thing about this is that all of these details are beyond the baby's control.

Those who struggle with favoritism for any of these reasons, must make a choice to let go of their unrealistic expectations, and begin elevating their unfavored child. They need to ask God to show them ways to love and build up this child who needs their full love and acceptance—as they do, they will discover that the child has unique strengths and qualities.

c. Reflecting the parents' flaws.

This is another cause of favoritism, or the reverse—unfavored treatment. Most of us are painfully aware of our own faults. Unfortunately, as we live day in and day out with our children, we get irritated if we see a child living out *our* flaws. Often seeing our flaws in a child magnifies our frustration. It's far better for us to deal with our own faults before we try to remove them from our child.

Regardless of our preconceived ideas or the flaws our child may possess, a sovereign God has placed a specific child in each family. Each child is an incredible gift, endowed with their own unique characteristics. A child who at first was a disappointment may be used by God to work off our rough edges.

Manifestations of Favoritism

Favoritism manifest itself three ways: *tone of voice*, *use of labels*, and *choice of gifts*.

a. Tone of voice.

This is very subtle. When I'm under pressure, my guard will drop, and I may speak sarcastically to one of my kids. I'm trying hard to take that cutting edge off of my words, but I don't always succeed. I have a ton of patience with the baby because I don't expect anything from her. But with my older children, at times of stress, I can slip into a disrespectful tone. The reason I'm working hard to correct it is that if a tone of disrespect continues, my children may start doubting that I respect them.

Among my acquaintances is a mother with two sons. One son is clearly her favorite, while the other consistently gets whatever is left over. I've been in her home when the sons are off at friends' houses and each will call to check in. The moment she answers the phone, I can instantly tell which son has called. If her favorite calls, she lights up and excitedly asks him how he's doing and wants to know all of the details. But when the unfavored son calls, she speaks slowly with a tone of hesitation or boredom. I doubt if this mother even recognizes it herself, but it is very subtle and very dangerous. Those boys know who is favored and who is not. The tone of voice reflects back to them their value and their worth.

b. Labels.

Favoritism can also be revealed in *labels*. If a mother is speaking of her daughter and says, "This is Susie, she's my good one." Well, another sibling standing nearby hears that and thinks, "I must be the bad one." Labels stick and can have a lasting impact.

Sometimes parents may jokingly label a child. This label many seem humorous to the parent, but to the child it may be very painful. In my home there was a joke about the end slices on a loaf of bread—they were called the "Bonnie ends." My father always thought it was very funny. Every few days as we used up another loaf of bread and they all would laugh about the Bonnie ends. But it wasn't funny to me. I would sadly think of those end slices as being the left overs, the pieces of bread that no one wanted. Protest as I might, I could not get them to stop this joke.

c. Choice of gifts.

A child, and even many adults, will look at gifts they receive as a measure of their worth—how important they are. If a child had a birthday party and no one brought a gift, the child would feel unloved. He would see the gifts as a tangible measure of his worth. I was recently at a child's birthday party and the mother told me that as the years passed, the gifts that came from grandma kept dropping in value. The mother was reading the long distance signs from her mother-in-law.

Be careful about your choice of gifts. Obviously all the kids do not want matching gifts, but be sure they are all of comparable worth or significance.

When Jacob gave Joseph the richly colored coat, it was proof to all the other brothers that Joseph was loved more than them. They had suspected it for many years and the coat was tangible proof to them. As a result their resentment grew into hatred.

3. Establish an intimate relationship with each child.

Every child comes into the world with basic emotional needs for love and acceptance. As a mother, I know my primary task is to guarantee that those needs are being met.

There may be days when the parent is on a downward spiral, and all she can see are the child's flaws. On days like that, the parent needs to step back emotionally and look logically at the child's strengths. They may not be readily evident, but they are there. Find his strengths and start building him up. Each child should be able to stand tall and know that he's loved and accepted. He should also be confident that he can make a significant contribution to the world.

With four children, I sometimes slip into the herd mentality where I see my children as a group. I need to take time to recognize their differences. If I take time to appreciate each one for his abilities, then each won't become jealous when I build up another child. They will each feel secure in their relationship with me.

4. Confront jealousy.

In the story of Rachel and Leah, Rachel was gorgeous. As a result, she was clearly favored by Jacob. For many years, however, she was infertile. In that culture a woman's worth was linked to her ability to produce many children. So Rachel was desperate to have a son. Meanwhile, Leah was desperate for Jacob's love and favor. God felt sorry for her and gave her six sons. This elevated her status significantly, but she was still consumed with winning Jacob's love. Both sisters had been blessed, but each was consumed with getting what the other sister had. As a result their individual blessings paled in comparison to what the other sister had.

Jealousy robs us of our joy. In our home, my first child struggles with jealousy toward my second. One day while we were at the park it escalated beyond reason. My older son was four at the time. He carried around four sticks. Apparently it's some type of boy ritual to pick up sticks and walk around banging tree trunks and bushes.

My second, who was two, walked around proudly carrying one stick like his big brother. The older son, however, was determined to get his brother's solitary stick. It didn't matter that he already had four in his hand. As I tried to get him to leave his brother alone, he persisted. In fact, he would have dropped all four of his sticks, just to claim the one from his brother. As I drove home, I knew I needed to do something to keep this from escalating further. I prayed and asked God for wisdom.

When I put my older son down for naptime, I sat by his bed and we talked. I told him about the word *jealousy* and tried to describe it in four-year-old terms. Since jealousy is commonly called the green-eyed monster, I told him all about the terrible green-eyed monster and how it gets inside a person and makes him miserable. I said it makes a person unhappy with what he has, and all he wants is what someone else has. The jealous person wants what other people have so much that it eats up his heart. All he can think about is getting what someone else has.

My son agreed that the green-eyed monster was terrible and he didn't want him to eat his heart. I explained about his jealous attitude toward his brother. He said he didn't want to be jealous anymore. So we prayed and he asked God to help him make the green-eyed monster go away.

Now, if your child struggles with nightmares or is easily scared, then you would be wise to describe a green-eyed cat or teddy bear who makes them sad or angry. The point is to make jealousy a tangible object that they can see in their imagination, so select something that would be appropriate for your child.

The next few days there was a marked change in his attitude toward little brother. Whenever I saw a jealous attitude emerging, I would tell him that the green-eyed monster was coming back. Often he would pray and ask Jesus to help him.

Most of the time he does well. When the jealousy emerges, we talk and often pray about it. This jealousy may never be completely gone, but we are keeping it under control.

5. Create a safe, fair environment.

Children need to know that home is a safe, fair place. Rules must be fair so smaller children aren't neglected. If children are left to themselves, the law of the jungle will prevail. The bigger, stronger child will get what he wants at the expense of the smaller ones. If this happens consistently, the younger will grow up thinking his desires aren't important, and won't expect anyone else to care about them either. This can be solved if they are given some basic rules of fair play. Rules about name calling, hitting, and sharing will protect the best interests of all the children.

Our rule about sharing is simple. When a child receives a new toy as a gift, he has exclusive rights to play with it. As time passes, the toy becomes community property and all freely play with it. If a child sees a sibling playing with his toy, he may suddenly decide he needs to play with it. Often, if it hadn't been picked up to be played with, it would still be sitting on the shelf collecting dust, but the rule of interest and demand takes over.

The rule for reclaiming a toy is to give the child a two minute warning that the owner would like his toy back. This gives the child two minutes to play and adjust to letting go. In a minute or two they hand it back to the owner. No screaming and no tears, because they treat each other with respect. Rarely does anyone need me to help enforce this rule.

In order to have a fair environment, the children need equal treatment as they reach milestones. I only have one child in school. We have his school photo sitting in a frame on our piano. One day my younger son looked at his brother's picture and asked why it was there. I said it was there to remind us of big brother while he was at school. His eyes lit up as he exclaimed, "When I go to school, then you will keep my picture on the piano, too!" He didn't feel any jealousy. He knew once he had crossed the same milestone he would receive the same treatment. Make sure that your children know beyond any doubt that Mom and Dad are equal opportunity parents.

6. Be fair in complimenting physical beauty.

The issue of physical beauty was a source of irritation between the sisters. Boys often care little about their physical appearance, but their athletic ability is usually very important. If the two daughters have different hair or eye color, or different height, the difference should be downplayed. If one girl is always hearing about her beautiful red hair, while the other with brown hair hears nothing, she will grow up feeling less important and beautiful. She may grow to deeply resent her sister.

If at all possible, when making a compliment to one child, try to give a compliment of equal importance to the other child when it is appropriate.

Whether we like it or not, beauty is an essential part of a girl's self-esteem and also impacts the way others view her. A mother should strive to enhance the natural features of each daughter. There is always a delicate balance between enhancing a girl's beauty and being obsessed with it.

As we look at beauty there are two types: internal and external. A woman will reach her physical peak between 19 to 25 years of age. But after age 26, the cosmetic industry makes millions off the rest of us as we try to keep the beauty from fading. Whether we like it or not, external beauty is fading.

If parents allow a daughter to focus heavily on her external beauty, so she becomes obsessed with her appearance, she will neglect developing internal character. She will also become disillusioned. One morning she will look in the mirror and find the years leaving their mark, as little wrinkles appear and then multiply.

It's far better to help her focus on developing internal beauty, the beauty of character and soul. This radiates from within. Like a good wine, it improves with age. Proverbs 30:31 says, "Charm is deceptive and beauty is fleeting; but a woman who fears the Lord is to be praised." Make sure your daughter has internal beauty. In the long run, this will lead to a fulfilling life.

7. Emphasize a lifelong relationship.

Since my children's relationships with each other will probably outlive my lifetime, I want to do all I can while they are young and establishing their relationships with one another to encourage harmony between them.

My dream is that one day when all of my children are grown and married, we will have big family reunions. We will spend Christmas in a big cabin in the snow. The kids, grandkids, and even the grandparents will have lots of fun playing in the snow, sledding and skiing. But if my children grow up fighting with each other, then when they are adults, they may not want to share a cabin. The happy reunions may dissolve into fighting and frustration.

There are families where the siblings barely speak to each other because some conflicts were never resolved. This can be prevented if the parents will seek to show kids how the other child is feeling, and thus instill more sensitivity toward each other. Parents must also be diligent to give children the long-range perspective. Siblings should see each other as teammates. Parents need to instill a team spirit so that the kids all belong together.

One day we were wading in a creek. We discovered some tiny minnows. My husband managed to catch one. Eventually we had three minnows swimming in our water bottle. As we caught each one, we named it for each of our children. We had *John fish*, *Gabriel fish*, and *Caleb fish* (the three fish brothers). I was ready to leave, and told

133

them it was time to go. "No!" they all shouted, "We still need an *Angela fish*!" They had a strong sense of identity with their baby sister and knew their fish family wouldn't be complete without her. Fortunately my husband managed to catch one more fish.

On days when I see tension mounting between the two oldest boys, I know it's time to develop a sense of camaraderie between them. I give them a task to do together. I might say, "I need you two big boys to go find the lost shoe." Or I might play a game like hide and seek with the two big boys on one team, while the two little ones and I try to find them. Giving them something to do together strengthens the bonds of unity. Later, when I see them run up the stairs together, off on some adventure, and hear them laughing or whispering about all their plans, I'm glad I made the effort to help them live in harmony.

Some years ago, a godly mother raised eight children who all grew up loving her and loving each other. She lived a long life and eventually died. After the funeral, all of the adult siblings gathered at her home. They sat around her living room and reminisced about her. They shared their favorite stories. Sometimes they laughed, sometimes they cried. Then the room grew silent. Finally one brother spoke up, "I'm not quite sure how to say this, but I always felt like an only child." Then a sister slowly spoke, "That's interesting, I always felt like an only child too." Then one by one each of the siblings said that they too had felt like only children. Somehow this mother had mastered the gift of developing an intimate relationship with each child. She made each one feel uniquely important to her.

I only have four and I feel it's a challenge to find time to develop an intimate relationship with each one. If this mother made time to do it with eight children—in a day before disposable diapers and washing machines—then I can do it too.

13

Attention Deficit Disorder

In recent years, much attention has been given to *Attention Deficit Disorder* (ADD). This is not a new phenomenon—it's a new name for an old problem. ADD has always influenced the way some people think and function, but in centuries past it did not have a name. In the recent past, "hyperactive" was used to describe a large majority of these children. Then educators introduced the term ADD (Attention Deficit Disorder) to describe the hyperactive child's deficient attention span. Once this term was used, educators noticed a whole subcategory of ADD children who were *not* hyperactive. So the term ADD was applied to all non-hyperactive children, while the term ADHD (Attention Deficit Hyperactive Disorder) was used to describe the vast majority of ADD children— all those who are hyperactive. For the sake of convenience, I will use the term ADD to encompass both ADD and ADHD children.

In the mid 1930's, a study was conducted with severely hyperactive children. Because their parents could no longer control them, they were put into a mental hospital for children with severe behavior disorders. The doctors' strategy with these children was tolerance. They reasoned that by showing tolerance, the children would feel respected and loved, so their problems would decrease. But in the days that followed they realized that all the tolerance wasn't helping. The children had shown no improvement.

The doctors' second strategy was to give the children individual psychotherapy, so they would know that the doctors really cared about each one of them. But they still saw no improvement. In desperation the doctors came up with plan C.

The third strategy created a constructive, restrictive, tolerant environment. The children were given constructive tasks so they felt a sense of purpose and accomplishment. The restrictive environment set boundaries for reasonable behavior so they would act more like normal children. When they overstepped these boundaries, they were put in isolation. Tolerance was used for minor offenses. This strategy was successful. It got to the point that many children began acting like normal children. They were released back to their homes. As long as the parents continued to create a constructive, restrictive, tolerant environment, the children continued to improve. Sadly, in many of the homes the parents were unable to provide the kind of environment required and the children regressed. They were committed to the mental hospital again.

Throughout this chapter, I will use the term ADD to encompass children struggling with ADD or ADHD. In education, the names change frequently. For now, the latest term is ADD.

What exactly is ADD?

ADD is the result of the brain's inability to accurately and consistently process all incoming data. Information in the brain is transmitted from cell to cell by chemicals called neurotransmitters. Since ADD children have such a difficult time processing information accurately and consistently, it is believed they are deficient in some neurotransmitters.

A simpler way of understanding this is to picture a light bulb. The energy source is in the outlet. A light bulb is dependent on the cord to carry the electricity from the outlet to the bulb. If there is a break in the cord, or a wire is frayed, the light will flicker. The flickering is the sign of the short-circuiting. So the characteristics of ADD are the outward symptoms of this internal malfunction.

ADD is the result of inborn temperamental differences in a child. How the child is treated and raised can effect the severity of the problem, but cannot cause it. Certain types of child rearing make it worse, other types make it better. No form of parenting can produce ADD in a child who is not temperamentally disposed to it.

The seven main characteristics of ADD are: distractibility or inattentiveness, impulsivity or lack of self-control, restlessness, perceptual and learning difficulties, social aggressiveness, hyperactivity, and poor eye-hand coordination. A child struggling consistently with five or more of these symptoms, may need to see a doctor in order to get an accurate diagnosis. ADD is a medical term and only a doctor can give a child the label. A parent or teacher, however, may recognize that a child

139

is struggling with several of these characteristics, regardless of whether they get a medical diagnosis or not. This chapter will give you a practical strategy for helping these struggling children to succeed.

At all times be very careful about using the label ADD in front of your child. Unfortunately, once a child hears it, he may be branded for life. He may use it as a cop-out for failure.

I call ADD the invisible disability. A blind or lame person can be readily spotted in our society, but the ADD person looks like everyone else. He just acts a little differently, and people often have trouble relating to him or understanding him.

Who has ADD?

Five million children in the United States have ADD. Three to ten percent of school-aged children have problems with ADD. This means in a class of thirty children, an average of one to three students will have ADD. Boys predominately struggle more with ADD, but some girls have it also.

The average ADD child is above average in intelligence.

Often a child with ADD will have SDD (Specific Developmental Disorder) which is the same thing as *Learning Disabilities* (of which dyslexia is one type.) A high percentage of children have both problems. Yet a few ADD children will not have SDD and vice versa.

How ADD Feels

Since many adults did not struggle with ADD as children, they will have difficulty understanding the child who does struggle. Once an adult can empathize with an ADD child, he will be better equipped to help him. But empathy should never become an excuse for allowing disobedience.

As a child who grew up with ADD, I have a lot of empathy for all of the misunderstood children who struggle with this problem. Because of short-circuiting in the brain, it's very difficult to focus attention appropriately. Since the child often feels bombarded with stimuli from several directions, the child finds it difficult, if not impossible, to concentrate and focus on the task at hand. This causes high levels of confusion. The child may often feel scatterbrained. This leads to feeling overwhelmed as the child fails to focus and complete the task. Often the child will notice an inability to do what everyone else around him or her can do. The child can't feel scattered and confused for very long before he grows frustrated. Out of frustration, whether in a home, playground, or classroom setting, the child will give up and thereby label himself a failure.

As the ADD child grows and peers develop more social sophistication, the child will have increasing problems fitting in socially. Because of the inability to focus and block out distractions in a social setting, the child will often be unable to read all of the subtle social cues being sent. This child soon gets labeled as "different," and may be ridiculed and shunned by peers. Meanwhile, the child is clueless about what is wrong, or what can be done to help him in this crucial area. Instead the child feels unlovable, unwanted, out of it, or distant from peers. This will be made worse if the child feels rejection from parents or teachers as well.

Pitfalls

Now that the problems of this child have been explained, there are five crucial pitfalls adults must avoid if they are to help this child.

1. Don't get angry.

Working with these children can be very stressful. To learn a new skill they may need ten times more help and repetition than their average peers. Since they may already be angry with themselves, they don't need the extra anger from an adult they respect. Instead, they need your patience. If you feel anger or frustration rising within, then give yourself and the child a break. After each person is calm and relaxed, come back to learning the skill and trying again. Even if a parent or teacher can control the tongue, if anger is oozing out of every action, the child will sense it and feel the rejection.

An adult's anger will not be constructive or productive. It will only undermine the relationship. The Apostle James reminds us in James 1:20, "For the anger of man does not achieve the righteousness of God" (NASB).

2. Never call the child names.

Once a child has been called stupid, dumb, slow, stubborn, or a klutz, that label will stick in a child's mind. The more the child hears it, the more it will stick, until the child is convinced he can never change. Since the parent or teacher is often on a pedestal, the child may even think that you walk on water. As a result, your words carry considerable weight. Set a guard on your mouth not to let anything derogatory slip from your mouth. If you feel yourself on the verge of insulting a child, turn around and walk away. Before those negative terms slip out.

If an adult calls a child a name, he may forget it the next day. But the child may remember it for a lifetime. I know adults today who are highly intelligent, but they've told me they're stupid. I've tried to convince them they're not, but they refuse to believe me. When they were children, someone carelessly gave them a label that has stuck for life.

3. Don't compare.

Never say, "Why can't you be more like . . .?" The ADD child spends her days encountering obstacle after obstacle. This child is already aware of the siblings and peers who are effortlessly sailing through life. The child knows she is different and would give anything to have their secret to success. When a child is compared to others, it merely heightens her own feelings of inadequacy and encourages her to feel jealous and resentful.

Instead get them to focus on personal improvement. "Yesterday you worked on your math paper for seven minutes without needing any help. Do you think you can work on it alone for eight minutes today? Let's set the timer and see how you do."

4. Don't use unrelated punishment.

Even though the child is having trouble focusing in the classroom, sending him out to sit in the hall won't help him. In fact, it will only hurt the child academically. When I was in second grade, I frequently spent time sitting out in the hall. I can still remember sitting in my little chair with no work to do, staring at the pattern of the wood grain on the shut door. I became the joke of the faculty and staff. "Are you out here again?" they would ask as they walked by shaking their heads. Thankfully, I didn't suffer too much academically and was able to pass second grade in spite of the lack of instruction and classroom time. This type of punishment was ineffective and could have been academically and emotionally damaging.

Instead of punishing me, the teacher should have helped me to stay focused. My desk should have been moved to a quieter part of the room, where the distractions were minimized, but I could still benefit from direct instruction. If that is done, the teacher should stress that the child isn't being punished, he is just sitting in a place where he won't be distracted. Once he can complete all his work and focus, he should be free to go back to his old spot.

If a child struggles with reversals, he shouldn't be punished academically. On any paper that contains reversals, the teacher should circle all reversals, and hand it back for the child to correct. A reversal must be fixed, but it shouldn't dock a child's grade.

5. Don't give up.

Once a child is labeled ADD, a parent or teacher may decide he is a hopeless case. This is not true. There are many successful adults who struggled with ADD as a child. In order to learn a new skill, the child may need tons of repetition. This child will have to work harder than his peers, but he will have his own unique strengths where he will excel if given the opportunity and encouragement.

A child must know that his parents and teacher are on his side. If they have faith in the child, he will make greater progress. Most ADD children can function in the regular classroom if they have the tools they need to compensate. The following strategies will help the child succeed.

Strategies To Build Success

Since working with an ADD child can be extremely stressful, an adult's first tactic must be prayer. God made this child, knows exactly how the child's brain functions, and what the child needs in order to achieve. The parent or teacher needs patience and wisdom as he seeks to help this hurting, frustrated child. Praying daily for patience and wisdom for the adult and asking God to help the child will bring great results. In the midst of a stressful confrontation, it's wise to stop again and pray for more wisdom and patience, and to pray that the child's mind would be opened and made clear. Here's an example.

Barbara was a busy student who consistently struggled with math. One day she was on the verge of exploding. I knew all of my efforts to teach her were not getting through. I quickly prayed for wisdom. Then it became clear that I needed to back away and allow her to cool off. I told her that I still wanted to help her but right now she needed to calm down. When she was calm and ready to learn, then she could come to my desk and ask me for help. I walked away asking the Lord to help her calm down. A few minutes later, she calmly came to my desk and asked for help. I showed her the new math skill and she got it.

Philippians 4:6 says, "Be anxious for nothing, but in everything by prayer and supplication with thanksgiving, present your requests to God." This verse can be very comforting during those tense moments when anxiety would be the natural response to the situation.

The following strategies will not only help your ADD child improve, but they're also good strategies to help any child improve. In addition to prayer, there are eight strategies for building success in a child: *routines, structured environment, academic, social, patience, perseverance, downward spirals*, and *sports*.

Consistent Routines

Since an ADD child is so distractible, a daily routine with lots of structure is needed. One of the main facets of the discipline system in this book has been to establish a structured home and classroom environment. This will help an ADD child considerably, yet the child needs additional structure as well.

Simple daily tasks like getting dressed can be difficult and time-consuming as the child often gets distracted. Moving from place to place, while trying to also dress, can be difficult for a child who keeps forgetting what should be done next. The child takes off his pajamas, goes into the bathroom, puts them in the hamper, returns to the room where he selects the necessary clothes from various dresser drawers. Then the child often needs to get pants and shoes from the closet. Not only can the ADD child be distracted at each point along the journey, but the child must also dress himself.

The number of steps necessary to complete the task increase the chance he will be distracted along the way. The simpler a parent can make this task, or any other that causes frustration, the more likely it is that the child will be able to complete it.

Any daily task can be taught to a child as a series of sub-tasks. Once the child masters this series of sub-tasks, always given in the same sequence, it will become a habit. It may be difficult to learn this habit, but once the child has it down, it will be mastered for life. It will be as if the child is on autopilot, gliding through the once frustrating task. Otherwise, the child struggles every day trying to reinvent the wheel. The child will be full of confusion and questions, saying, "Now, should I put my pajamas in the hamper first, or should I put on my socks first, or . . .?"

It may be helpful to make a list chronologically, with all of the sub-tasks in order. Then the child can look at the list each morning and know what to do next. Mom will no longer need to nag him or follow him around. This type of list may also be helpful for bedtime or any other daily routine that creates a lot of frustration.

The more a child successfully completes daily routines, the less frustrated the child will be, and more time will be left to focus on the bigger things in life. Once the child successfully masters his daily routine, the chart will no longer be necessary.

This is also true for the classroom. The more a teacher helps a child to break a large task into several small predictable sub-tasks, the sooner the child will be able to concentrate on the more important task of learning.

In my classroom, the routine was the same every day. The children would hang up their backpacks, put away their lunches, return any homework, and sit down at their desks. They got out a pencil and paper and started writing their spelling sentences. Meanwhile I quietly walked around the room rewarding the ones who were quietly working on their work. Since every child knew exactly what to do, they all developed the habit of getting started in the morning, so we didn't waste any precious class time.

Firm, consistent, predictable rules will give the ADD child the boundaries he needs to thrive.

If a child is constantly losing things, then he will need help getting his room or desk organized. If a student keeps losing his pencil or eraser, take a look in his desk. It will probably look like a hazard zone. During the next available recess, have him stay in and clean out his desk. Help him organize it. When he is all done tell him how nice it looks. Remind him that every time he puts a pencil back, it should go in the same spot, then he will be able to find it the next time. Then ask him if he can keep it looking nice until the end of the day. Tell him you will be sure and check.

Structured Environment

Distractions are a major obstacle for the ADD child, so the environment in the classroom and at home should minimize distractions. There are three main sources of distractions: visual clutter, noise, and movement.

The Classroom

The environment for work time should be as close to silent as possible. Other children may not need this much silence to successfully do their work, but an ADD child must have it to function. If the windows look out on the playground while other classes are at recess, the ADD child will have difficulty focusing on the teacher when he could be watching the big kids play soccer. It is very easy for the teacher to close the curtains until recess is over.

Visual clutter should be kept to a minimum. Wild, bright bulletin boards and art projects suspended from the ceiling may be exciting and stimulating to the students, but they are too simulating to the ADD child, who may be unable to focus on anything but the bulletin boards and art projects. If necessary, move the ADD child to a boring part of the classroom.

Movement in the room may also be very distracting, so the child's desk needs to be on an edge of the desk arrangement—preferably in the front, away from obvious traffic patterns. Removing her from the group should only be done if she is unable to function within the group. She still needs to be placed where she can see and hear any instructions given. She also needs to be told why she is being moved—that she is being moved to cut down on distractions, so it will be easier for her to focus on her work. *Stress that the child is not being punished.*

The Home

At home, visual clutter, noise, and movement will also hamper a child trying to do homework. Create a quiet working place, preferably in a room where the child can be alone. A desk or table top, facing a blank wall in a well-lit corner will have the least distractions. While the child is studying, siblings must keep out and make their noise elsewhere. If there is a lot of outside noise, some soft classical music may help to block these distractions and be soothing, too.

Even in college, I was unable to study in my dorm room if my roommate came in and was silently moving about in the room. I found the only place I could really study was in a study booth in a remote corner of the library.

Strengthening Academic Skills

As stated earlier, not all ADD children will have SDDs (Specific Developmental Disorders) or Learning Disabilities, but there is a high percentage of ADD kids who also have SDD. As a result, the child with both disorders will need extra academic help. First, the parent or teacher needs to study the child carefully and discover how he learns.

People process information mainly through auditory or visual channels to the brain. Often a child will have a dominant channel. Once the dominant channel is discovered, the parent or teacher needs to focus on teaching the child through the best channel. A strong auditory child needs to hear the teacher explain the rules, even if they're written across the top of the page. On the other hand, a strong visual child needs to see the directions written, even though the teacher may have spoken them to the class. A wise teacher will give directions several ways to enhance understanding.

A daily link between home and school must be established if the child is struggling academically. A necessary item is a steno notebook in which the child records his daily assignments, highlighting the completed ones, and noting those that are unfinished. In order to assure accuracy, the teacher should sign the notebook at the end of the day, and the parent should sign it when the homework is complete. If they need to communicate further, they can write notes back and forth in the same notebook.

In order to enforce this daily record of assignments, the parents may either dock the child's allowance for forgetting, or give the child a smaller allowance with a bonus for each day that the child remembers. At all times, the child is responsible for updating this book. It is not the teacher's job to hound the child each day. It would be nice for the teacher to help the child start the new habit with a reminder at the end of each day for a week or two, but then it should be up to the child. A parent should check for the notebook the minute the child is picked up at school, and if he has forgotten it, the child needs to go back to the room and get it.

The child with both ADD and SDD should be studied carefully to determine her strengths and weaknesses. This is done to encourage the child's strengths and develop strategies to help her cope with weaknesses.

Strengths.

It is necessary to focus on a child's strengths first in order to build up self-confidence. By the time a child is recognized as having ADD, he has already had several setbacks and may consider himself a failure. This child needs to find out he is really good at something. Nothing breeds success like success. Words of encouragement are nice, but if the child feels dumb or like a failure inside, the words will have little impact. Instead, the child needs to know that he is great at singing, acting, or science.

Since a teacher sees dozens, maybe hundreds of children of the same age, she is in a good position to recognize a child who is outstanding. One of my students made beautiful pictures with careful details and excellent proportions. I told her mother she was gifted in art, and encouraged her to provide an opportunity for lessons. Later when she was in college, she spent some time in

151

Scotland perfecting her painting skills. I'm glad I took the time to notice.

Every child will have strengths. Often the child's weaknesses will be blaring at an adult. The adult needs to look carefully to find two areas of strength. A parent should select the child's two greatest strengths and provide opportunities, if possible, for him to take lessons so he can excel.

There is an old phrase, "You gotta lather before you shave." Once we build them up, they will have more confidence to face their weaknesses.

Weaknesses

A parent or teacher should next focus on a child's two lowest areas. These weaknesses are causing the most failure for the child, so they should be dealt with first. If possible, the adult should pinpoint the exact cause of the problem. This will require the adult to play detective. Then the teacher or parent needs to give the child tools to compensate by learning to work around the problem. For example, if a child misses a lot of addition problems on one assignment, but performs well on another page, the two papers should be compared. Look for clues to success or failure. Maybe the good page listed all the problems in columns, while the problem page listed the problems horizontally. A child with problems tracking could have considerable problems with such a page. If possible, remedy this situation by only giving math problems in columns, or perhaps the parent could rewrite the problems in columns.

When I was in fourth grade, our math textbook showed a problem and included a small square box for the answer. These books were not meant to be written in, so the boxes were quite small. Even though I was strong in math, suddenly I found myself growing very frustrated as I tried desperately in my mind to find an answer small enough to fit in the little box on the page. I am sure my teacher never knew how frustrating those boxes were to me, and I never knew to tell her.

Often the visual layout of the page may be very difficult for a child, and may cause so much stress, that she is prevented from successfully completing the task. The child needs an understanding adult to help her surmount these obstacles, by finding the cause of difficulty, and helping the child successfully work around it. In reading, a child may struggle with keeping her place. If she loses her place frequently, the child needs to use a bookmark under each line of print. This will improve the tracking considerably.

All the math facts must be memorized by rote. If a child is strongest auditorally, he should practice memorizing them by saying them aloud (better yet, a parent or older sibling could quiz him by saying them aloud, then he also hears someone else saying them). A strong visual child should see the math facts (use flash cards) and write the answer so he can see it. Whichever way a child learns best, the more channels that can deliver the information to the brain, the better the child's chances for success. Math facts must become so ingrained, that the child can give the correct answer out of habit.

As with learning any new skill, start with small goals only the "two" multiplication tables until they are habit. Then move on to the "threes" until they are habit. Review the "twos" frequently. Continue in this way until all the multiplication tables have been learned. The car is an excellent place for review of this sort. The goal of all of this review, is to move the vital information out of the short-term memory of the brain and into the long-term memory. Then the child will have these facts for life.

If the child has been struggling for long in any academic area, then he should be evaluated to determine if there are areas where he needs remediation. Most learning consists of a hierarchy of skills. This means that a simple skill is taught first. Once it is mastered, a slightly more complex skill is taught based on the knowledge learned in the first skill. This process of learning continues, growing more complex at each level. If a child fails to master a simpler skill, he will not be able to move onto higher levels successfully. Thus the need for remediation, going back and fixing any problems in the hierarchy of learning.

Make learning as fun as possible. If you can, think of a way to turn it into a game. This will make it seem less tedious and the child will be more open to learning. The more fun and exciting anything is, the more eager a child will be to learn. In fact they may not even realize they are learning, because they are too busy having fun. When the parent or teacher hits a roadblock, and the child is just not understanding, then it is time to stop and cool off before the adult or child loses their temper. Come back later, when both are relaxed, and work on it in small time increments, gradually increasing the amount of time and, hopefully, level of progress.

Developing Social Skills

Even though an ADD child may do well academically, most of them, will struggle socially. Social success or failure will influence a child's happiness in life. Because of the distractions and unnecessary stimuli bombarding a child every day, an ADD child cannot pick up the subtle social cues other people send. Even as an adult, I find I still pick up new social subtleties that I have been blind to all my life.

When an adult observes a situation where the ADD child fails socially, she needs to take the child aside privately and point out the blind spot. Help the child to understand the other person and why things happened the way they did. Help the child read social cues by heightening his people-reading skills. Point out specific body language, like arms crossed across the chest and feet firmly planted on the ground to explain that the child's listener was becoming angry and defensive. Explain that as soon as the child sees someone act like that, he would be wise to back off and drop the topic. Explain how verbal cues like silence on the part of the listener and eyes that wander, show that the listener is tired of listening. The ADD child would be wise to stop talking as soon as he sees this to prevent boring the listeners further.

Often these children are socially aggressive— everyone else has learned to be subtle, except them. If this is the case, they need to learn to talk less and watch and listen more. The milk commercials that say, "Milk, good fast food," feature a man who intrudes on parties and talks too much. He is an excellent example of a socially aggressive person. Nobody likes him. Socially aggressive people should learn to walk into a social setting, be still for five minutes and just observe the atmosphere, and then carefully plan what they want to say and who they want to say it to. They need to learn to ask questions of others and then wait to listen to the answer. Teach them that *yes or no* questions aren't good for aiding conversation, and that they should ask *what and when* questions that give people an opportunity to expound. The more a child learns to focus on others rather than himself, the more successful he will be socially.

Patience

In order to overcome impulsive behavior, a child must develop patience and self-control. These may take a lifetime to perfect, but the child must learn some basic self-control. A major cause of impulsive behavior is shortsightedness and the inability to think long-term. This causes a child to flit from one thing to the next. Whenever the child hits an obstacle, or becomes bored, she moves on to something else, leaving a series of unfinished tasks in the wake. This child needs to develop delayed gratification. This means the child must learn to delay personal gratification or pleasure until a long and possibly cumbersome task has been finished. Then she will have the reward when it is over.

Teaching this is not easy, but it may be done gradually, starting with small tasks and giving a reward upon their completion. Slowly, the length of time necessary to complete the task is increased before the reward is received. The reward should grow in proportion to the size of the task. Many of the important things in life depend on this skill of delaying gratification. A full-time salary straight out of high school may look tempting to some kids, yet the four years of study necessary to earn a college degree will yield greater rewards if the child can be patient that long.

An excellent way to teach a child this concept is through the use of a token economy. In a token economy, a child earns tokens for good behavior. In advance, the child should be told what specific actions or chores will earn him a token. These tokens can be used as currency in exchange for rewards. One token can buy 15 minutes of TV, candy, a sticker, or some other small reward. Ten tokens can buy a special trip to Baskin & Robbins with the parent of his choice—or some other mid-sized reward. Soon the child will realize the smart use of tokens is to save them and work toward big rewards. If the child earns ten tokens and uses them up immediately he may have ten M&M's, one at a time; but if he saves them, the child can go out to Baskin and Robbins, which is far better. Once the child easily saves ten tokens, the parent might think of better rewards for 25 tokens—like having a friend spend the night, or a day at the zoo.

Perseverance

Since an ADD child has a harder time than most when learning new skills, she must learn to persevere even in the face of obstacles. Thomas Edison—who was severely SDD, and therefore probably ADD—said after repeatedly failures in trying to develop a light bulb, "Well, I now know 1000 ways not to make a light bulb." That's determination. In spite of his own difficulties, he did not quit. Winston Churchill said it so well, "Never give up. Never, never, give up!" To be successful, that *must* be the battle cry of an ADD child.

As a Christian parent or teacher, we have the added bonus of helping this child tap into the most powerful source of all, the almighty Creator of the universe. When the child is frustrated and ready to quit, the child can pray and ask God to help open his or her mind. The more the child develops this habit of prayer when struggling, the more the child will feel God at work in his life and the more obstacles he will be able to surmount.

The child should be encouraged to memorize Scripture, enabling her to think on it at times when she is tempted to quit. Isaiah 42:16 is an excellent verse. "I will lead the blind by ways they have not known, along unfamiliar paths I will guide them; I will turn the darkness into light before them and make rough places smooth. These are the things I will do; I will not forsake them." Philippians 4:13 says, "I can do everything through Him who gives me strength." And James 1:5 says, "If any of you lacks wisdom, he should ask God, who gives generously to all without finding fault, and it will be given to him."

Stopping Downward Spirals

As parents and teachers begin to know the child better, they may be able to predict what settings usually spark a downward spiral of out-of-control behavior. An observant parent will quickly spot the early symptoms and attempt to head off an outburst before it happens. Either the parent should attempt to have the child avoid such settings, or should remove the child as soon as possible. When a parent knows of certain unavoidable problem settings in advance, the child should be spoken to privately, before entering the setting, and told exactly what is expected and what reward or punishment can be expected.

Sports

Eye-hand coordination is a typical problem for half of all ADD children, so they may struggle with clumsiness and feel awkward with sports. This is especially painful for boys since their worth and acceptance by peers can depend heavily on athletic ability. Sports, like baseball and tennis, that require tracking a bouncing ball may be near to impossible for the ADD child. On the other hand, track, swimming, and football require speed and endurance, which may be mastered by an uncoordinated child.

Conclusion

Working with the ADD child to develop strategies to compensate for the child's weaknesses may be a very long and slow process, one that can take years. But every ounce of effort put into helping this child will pay pounds of dividends as he moves successfully into adolescence and adulthood. The child may still have obstacles, but will have the tools to fight and win.

Since ADD has a genetic link, often as a parent discovers about his child's struggles, the parent may see himself, too. If he is still struggling as an adult, the tactics used to help the child may also help him. Fortunately, half of all who suffer with ADD outgrow it by the time they reach adulthood. Currently, there are 10 to 15 million adults with ADD in the United States.

14
Cultivating Character

Discipline is far more than punishing a child. The highest purpose in discipline is to instill godly character traits. As a mother, my primary goal is to develop godly character traits in my children that will be a part of them throughout life. If my children become successful by the world's standard but are spiritually bankrupt, I will have failed to pass on that which I treasure above all else. Before godly character traits can be cultivated, however, a parent must prepare for growth.

Cultivating Character

Cultivating character in a child is much like cultivating plants in a garden. I grew up in Washington state on the edge of open farmlands. Each summer, all of us kids were supplied with seeds and our own plot of dirt. All I had to do was dig some holes, plant the seeds, and water daily. In no time healthy green shoots broke through and reached toward the sun. Then my garden became more exciting as I watched the progress of each plant. Before long, I harvested carrots and other vegetables. That was the best part.

Later, as an adult, I had fond, carefree memories of my gardening days. The spring after we bought our first home in Silicon Valley, I planted a full vegetable garden. I watered it daily and eagerly waited for little green shoots to appear. Once they did, I was elated. I had finally become a gardener in my own yard. Within a few weeks, however, I noticed that several vegetables never even grew into shoots and that many of my shoots struggled to grow at all. I continued to water and hoped for the best. By August, my pitiful little garden contained some green onions and miniature corn stalks that produced dwarfed ears of two-inch corn. My only consolation was a few green bean plants that bravely produced normal green beans. On a good day, I could harvest up to seven beans!

Needless to say, I had taken gardening for granted. After all, it had been so easy when I was young. Strong healthy plants need far more than water to thrive. So it is with children.

I am saddened to see so many teens today who have turned out angry and confused. The crime rate among our teens is rising. Children are now murdering other children. During the writing of this book there were several stories in the newspaper about two 10- and 11-year-olds in Chicago who pushed a five-year-old out of a 14th story window because he refused to steal candy for them. Such horrors aren't limited to big cities anymore, they're even happening in small, rural towns.

The parents of the children who commit such terrible crimes may have grown up in a simpler era, and had the same view of child rearing that I had about gardening—

just add water and everything will thrive. But they found out that life wasn't as simple as they had once thought. The price I paid for learning my lesson was insignificant. The price these parents have paid is too deep to fathom. Raising emotionally healthy children isn't random or automatic, it requires diligent effort.

So what went wrong with my Silicon Valley garden? As I admired my neighbors' thriving gardens and asked for their secrets, they all said the same thing: "You need to prepare the soil." Now this was all new to me. I never knew dirt could be so important.

Home Conditions

Just as soil conditions must be right for a healthy plant to thrive, so the home conditions must be right for healthy children to thrive. Four aspects that contribute to healthy home conditions are: *preparing for growth, establishing a solid marriage, modeling,* and *daily quiet time.*

Preparing for growth

Every successful gardener knows that long before he plants a seed, he must prepare the soil. This can be hard, tedious labor as he breaks up the soil, removes rocks and weeds, and applies fertilizers. This is so easy to overlook and yet is a crucial factor for success. Even the Bible tells us in Jeremiah 4:3, "Break up your fallow ground, And do not sow among thorns."

Parents who prepare their home conditions—or environment—before children come along are at a definite advantage. The younger a child is, the easier it will be to make plans for her. It may take weeks or months before a seed grows big enough to break through the ground. This time for the seed is crucial to the success of the plant. As the soil completely surrounds the tender budding seed, so the baby or small child is completely influenced by her home environment. This time of complete influence lasts until the child begins preschool or school.

I know a couple who make yearly plans to cultivate godly character traits in their children. They look at each child individually and make plans for encouraging certain traits while discouraging negative traits they want to eliminate. Another friend, Lisa, is a school teacher who makes weekly lesson plans. She now makes character plans for her daughters. These parents are living out the truth of a wise maxim: "If you fail to plan, you plan to fail."

Establishing a healthy marriage

According to the 1993 Census, 25 percent of American children live in single-parent homes. That means 75 percent of America's children live with two parents. Of those two-parent homes, a healthy marriage is not an option, it's a necessity.

My friend, Melba, is a godly, mature mother who has raised four committed Christian children that are all very close to her and to each other. One day I asked for her secret in mothering. She wisely replied, "A healthy marriage must come first. They all know my husband and I deeply love each other." She took me off-guard with her statement. *A successful mother must first be a successful wife.*

As I pondered this, I thought of several homes where I had seen the reverse—where children were the first priority and the marriage was second. The prevailing attitude in many marriages seems to be, "Raising small children is an all-consuming job, and I devote far more time to meeting the needs of my little ones than I give to meeting my husband's needs. After all, he's an adult and can tie his own shoes."

The real issue, however, is where do my priorities lie? The marriage must be top priority. Husband and wife were meant to meet each other's emotional needs. If a mother or father begins to look to the child to meet his or her emotional needs, then problems will arise. Usually a strong father/daughter or mother/son alliance will develop that can divide the family. A parent's emotional needs can never be fully met by a child, and more important, it is very unhealthy for a child to feel the burden of trying to meet his parent's needs. That weight is too great for him.

Genesis 27 gives the sad story of Isaac and Rebekah's distant marriage and the alliance each parent had with a child. This divided family acted like two teams bent on beating the other. None of the players were happy or had their needs met. Keeping a healthy marriage during the stressful time of raising children may be hard work, but it's worth it for the good of everyone involved.

Modeling character

The next spring when I was ready to plant again, I asked my neighbor, Nancy, who had a thriving garden, for help. I listened to what she said, but also watched what she did and carefully matched her efforts in my own garden. She became my model gardener. So it is with children: they are watching every move we make. I never would have taken Nancy's gardening tips seriously if she had a pathetic garden. So children will be resistant toward efforts to build character in them, if those same character traits are lacking in the parent. A child will unconsciously pattern himself after the parent. If I am living out consistent godly character before my kids, they will develop similar character.

Dr. Howard Hendricks says, "Every man has two sets of convictions. Christian convictions are written on paper—what he ought to do. Real convictions are written on his life—what he does." It will be impossible to teach my child honesty if I tell a "white lie" to a friend. Little eyes and ears are soaking up everything. If they see hypocrisy in me, my children will reject my efforts to instill godly character in them.

Daily quiet time

This crucial task of passing on the torch to the next generation can become overwhelming. Fortunately, we have ready access to the great God of this universe. He cares about our concerns and wants to give us wisdom as we face this task. Daily prayer enables us to link into His power when we feel all worn out. Daily Bible reading is God's way of speaking to us and giving us the wisdom we need. Prayer and Bible study are like a two way conversation. Through prayer we speak to God, and through Bible study God speaks to us. He loves our children even more than we do. My friend, Martha, says, "Jesus wants to be our parenting partner."

Nurturing Relationships with Water and Sunlight

As the little seedling in the garden continues to grow, it must be nurtured with regular water and sunlight. So also the child needs regular nurturing by developing a close, affectionate relationship with each parent.

My children don't care how much I know, until they know how much I care about them. Yes, I must tell my children I love them, but talk is cheap. They also need to see how much I love them through my actions.

Children need our time. The *Children's Defense Fund* of Washington, DC, reports that almost 20 percent of the children ages 6 to 12 in the United States haven't had even a ten-minute conversation with a parent in a month's time. Spending time together in front of the TV, or riding together in the car listening to music, doesn't encourage bonding because no one is communicating. They are merely coexisting. Time spent talking, hugging, and laughing will build a strong bond.

A friend named Gail noticed whenever she stopped whatever she was doing in response to her son's request to play with him, he was overjoyed to have her playing with him. Often at these times, he would spontaneously exclaim, "Mommy, I love you so much!"

One day she told her husband that she had noticed this trend. That evening the son asked his father to play with him. The father put down his newspaper and played with his son. While they were playing, the son spontaneously announced, "I love you Daddy!" In a situation like this, *everyone wins*.

Children also need our interest. Whenever I build a friendship, I must listen to my friend and express interest in her interests. So it is with my children. Life is very busy. It's easy to be caught in the busyness of completing all my daily tasks, which need to be done. But I need to set aside time for little interruptions, like the freshly picked dandelion from the yard that comes full of love.

Children need to be enjoyed for who they are. If I listen with interest to my son's latest escapades with the imaginary pirates in our backyard, he knows I care about what's important to him. Children know we *love* them, but they also need to know we *like* them. If he knows beyond a doubt that I am interested in him alone, and not just interested in his achievements, he will feel my love and be open to moral instructions.

Bad Influences of Pests

The next year in my garden, I was ready to try again. Before I planted, we worked hard preparing the soil, breaking up the hard ground, and removing rocks. Then I planted my garden carefully following all the directions on the seed packets. In no time I had lots of green shoots breaking through the soil.

Then one morning I found a bunch of my green shoots were gone. I rushed to the phone and asked my neighbor, Nancy, what went wrong. She asked if I had any snails and sowbugs in my yard. I said I did. She said they had eaten my tender shoots. One night of feasting had nearly destroyed my garden. Snails and sowbugs became my greatest enemies. I declared all-out war on those hungry intruders.

Similarly, bad influences can quickly undermine a parent's careful cultivation. Parents must guard children from bad influences. You can start by focusing on three potentially negative influences in your child's life: *other children, entertainment*, and *adults*.

1. Other children

A young child is highly vulnerable. He shouldn't be expected to reform the child next door, especially if that child is negatively influencing him. As syndicated columnist, Cal Thomas says, "There are no eight-year-old ambassadors." Before someone can become an American ambassador, he must grow into a solid American citizen and be well acquainted with our culture and constitution. In the same way, a child must be firmly rooted in his Christian faith before he can think of reforming others. If a child tries to influence another child and pull him up, chances are greater that the other child will wrongly influence him and pull him down.

If a child is wrongly influencing my child, I will prevent my child from being with him. I will not allow another child to undermine what I am trying to instill in my own. A friend, Roselynn, volunteered in her son's classroom each week. She observed the kids, and decided which ones she wanted her son to play with. Her son wanted to play with "Mr. Cool," but she knew this boy got into a lot of trouble. So she tried to discourage her son from playing with him. She kept emphasizing the two boys who had the right character qualities. One night near the end of the year, he said to his mother, "I think you're right, the cool kid is always getting into trouble." The other two boys became his friends.

2. Entertainment

Entertainment encompasses all the information a child may encounter. This includes television, books, magazines, comic books, video games, movies, videos, and music. None of these mediums is inherently bad, but all have great influence over little eyes, ears, and minds. The younger a child is, the more impressionable. If he is allowed to view or hear questionable material at a young age, it will warp his perspective. If he is exposed to graphic, violent material, it will create in him a desire to see more. A wise parent will screen all material before a child sees it. A child's innocence is fragile. Once it's lost, it cannot be regained.

There's a computer expression, "Garbage in—garbage out." If children are exposed to garbage, it will come out in their actions.

The influence of television can never be underestimated. Children watch an average of 23.5 hours of television each week. One morning while my son was watching Barney, the theme song started. "I love you, you love me . . . With a great big hug and a kiss from me to you." I was shocked to see him get up and hug the television as Barney sang. If an imaginary dinosaur can have that much influence over my son, I must make sure that what he sees on television is wholesome and encourages solid morals.

3. Adults

A young child is highly susceptible to the wrong influence of adults he admires. So make sure his neighbors and his friends' parents are good examples. And, if there is ever an adult who makes you feel suspicious or uneasy, avoid him or her and keep your children away. There are too many twisted people in our society today. Often after a perverted serial killer is caught and put in jail, news reporters will go to his neighbors and ask if they ever suspected him. The standard answer is, "No, he was a nice quiet man who kept to himself."

This isn't said to scare parents, but to remind moms that if their women's intuition—it may also be the Holy Spirit—causes them to be cautious about someone, they should act on that caution and keep themselves and their children away.

Protecting a Child's Heart

There is a five-step strategy for protecting a child's heart.

1. Shield him as long as possible.

There is no rush to tell them all the facts of life early. When children ask questions, the parents should give them age-appropriate answers. Before children reach puberty, however, they should hear the basic facts of life from their parents—not from their peers.

2. Enjoy the latency stage.

In the world of child development, the pre-kindergarten to elementary years (ages 4-12) are known as the *latency stage*. At this stage, children are beyond potty training and a preoccupation with gender types. These are the years of innocence when sexual development is latent. Boys are free to pursue all the normal interests like sports and bugs. Girls are free to pursue all their normal interests like ballet or art. They are free to merely be children without all the concerns of adulthood that will come soon enough.

3. Lost innocence can't be regained.

Once a child is exposed to something, it won't readily be forgotten. A child who is exposed to graphic sexual material will develop an appetite for more. The more a child is exposed to, the sooner he will be forced along the continuum toward adulthood. He will be a child physically and emotionally with the drives of an adolescent. This is very unhealthy. Once children pass informational milestones, they can not return to the carefree days of innocence. But this doesn't need to be a tragedy. A wise parent will do what they can to redeem the situation.

4. Talk through all the details.

Regardless of where or how your child was exposed to graphic sexual information, you need to get all the details. Chances are very good that it will be inaccurate information, at best. Ask questions to make sure you understand the full picture.

5. Share God's eternal perspective.

Once all the details have been gathered, try to view the situation from an eternal perspective. Ask your child what God thinks about it. Always bring it back to God as the ultimate authority, and not merely mom and dad. Then look at why it is wrong. Help the child to see the long term physical and emotional consequences of illicit sexual activity. Also talk about all the long-term benefits of abstinence until marriage.

Planting Instructions

Every seed packet comes with specific instructions for planting. They tell you how deep to plant the seed and how far apart to space them. When you plant the right seeds in the right way, the right plants will grow. So it is with children—so here are four basic instructions or techniques for instilling the seeds of godly character. They are: *be a strong role model, use lessons from life, encourage*, and *correct*.

1. Be a strong role model.

The example a parent sets is what the children will follow. This has been mentioned before, but it cannot be overemphasized. When I fail, however, it's not the end of the world. I tell my children I'm sorry, I admit it was wrong to lose my temper and yell at them, and then I ask for their forgiveness. They are always ready to forgive me. The act of humbly admitting I was wrong makes them melt. It resolves the problem, and they are eager to move on.

Even today, when my husband is about to make a big decision, he will often ask himself, "What would my parents or grandparents do in this situation?" They were good role models and made a big impact on his life. I hope that one day when my children are grown, they will ask the same question. Better yet, maybe they will even call on the phone and ask.

2. Use lessons from life.

Life is full of lessons, if we only open our eyes to see them. Deuteronomy 6:7 talks about sharing God's truth, "And you shall teach them diligently to your sons, and shall talk of them when you sit in your house and when you walk by the way and when you lie down and when you rise up." This tells us to weave God's truth, His principles, into our daily life as we talk with our children. This isn't just a five minute talk each night after dinner.

A modern translation of this verse could be, "Teach your children when you walk along the way or drive along the freeway." One day it occurred to me that the time spent in the van was usually wasted time. I decided it would be good to pass on some sort of oral tradition. I want the children to learn from my mistakes. I share childhood stories about times when I got in trouble and learned a lesson. The kids enjoy this transparency as they look into the world of mother as a little girl. My kids love these stories so much, that often when an aunt, uncle, or grandparent rides with us in the van, the kids immediately ask them to tell stories about when they were little and *did something wrong*.

Lessons from your life will be eagerly received by your children. It's fun for them to hear about you as a child. Stories about a time when you did something wrong, and learned from the consequences, will be received more readily than stories from books. Sin often offers immediate benefits, but ends with long-term pain. Help your children to see sin in its full light. We can learn so much from our mistakes, and by sharing them with our children perhaps we can prevent them from making the same mistakes.

Lessons from other lives are also useful. The Bible is full of stories about people and the lessons they learned. The good thing about Scripture is that it exposes people for who they really are, warts and all. Scripture always puts sin in its full context, so we can see the final result of wrong actions. This will help to counteract the Hollywood and TV glamorizing of wrong actions and failure to show the true results.

Our founding fathers were godly men with outstanding character. George Washington and Abraham Lincoln are wonderful men who teach many lessons through their lives. There are also biographies of many great heroes of the faith. It's good for children to have heroes, but they must have the right ones—hopefully, those who are godly men and women, past and present.

Teachable moments are a third type of lesson. When a situation happens, and the child's interest is heightened, seize the opportunity to teach a lesson. A friend, Janine, was walking into a video store with her nine-year-old son. A gang of teenage boys were loitering in front of the store. After my friend and her son walked back out to their car, he asked his mother why the teens were standing around. She told him that they were bored and didn't have anything else to do, so they stood there looking tough and frightening customers. Her son thought about this a moment and then said, "When I get to be big like them, I'll be too busy to stand around. I'll be busy playing baseball and soccer." It would have been easy for his mother to say, "Just don't pay any attention to boys like that." But instead she made it a teachable moment and he learned a valuable lesson.

3. Encourage.

When you see the first little shoots of godly character emerge in your child's life, encourage him. If he's been mean to a sibling, and then he gives his brother a cookie before taking one for himself, make a big deal of his generosity. If you'll take time to notice those little acts of kindness and make encouraging comments about them, they'll become a habit in your child's life.

4. Correction.

Correction is the weeding and pruning to eliminate anything that's preventing growth. For instance, as you seek to instill honesty in your child, lies will prevent honesty from taking root. So lies must be dealt with immediately whenever you discover one. Pull them out of your child's character, and honesty will increasingly prevail.

Seeds of Character Traits

Now we will finally look at the actual seeds we want to plant. The seeds are the character traits we want to develop in our child's life.

As we look more closely at seeds, each is unique. Each has a distinct genetic code. A watermelon seed will only produce watermelons. As we seek to instill godly character traits in our children, we must look closely at the distinct essence of each trait. The planting techniques give us a four-pronged approach for planting. The more techniques you use as you instill each character trait, the greater the final result.

The list of character traits could be endless. I have selected nine that I am working to instill in my children. They are: *a heart for God, kindness, integrity, responsibility, discernment, confidence, contentment, patience*, and *perseverance*.

1. A heart for God.

Jesus said the greatest command was to love God with all your heart, mind, and soul. Just as my greatest devotion must be for God, so I want each of my children to give their greatest devotion to God. If our children's highest allegiance is to God, then God will help them stand true to their convictions when teen pressure is intense. Children's loyalty to God will keep them on the right path much longer than loyalty to parents alone.

Two or three weeks before my son started kindergarten, I gave him the standard pep talk about the start of school. When I asked him if he was excited about starting kindergarten, he asked, "Does God like Canterbury?" I reassured him that since it was a Christian school where they taught the Bible and prayed, God was happy with the school. I hope he will continue to ask that question as he makes life's choices. Wanting God's opinion before making a decision will help him avoid much heartache.

Our world is full of good things that could easily diminish our primary devotion to God. If the Superbowl is featuring my home team and the game is scheduled during our regular evening church service, I'm faced with a dilemma. Should I choose to show allegiance to God or the home team? My children will remember my choice long after I have forgotten the final score of the big game. Besides, in an age of VCRs this doesn't need to be an issue.

Anything that threatens to keep God from His rightful place in our home must be abandoned. I need to demonstrate my devotion to God in how I spend my money (Do I tithe?), time (Is regular church attendance a priority?), and talents (Do I use them in ministry?) This is the surest way of guaranteeing that my children will also be devoted to God.

2. Kindness.

Jesus said the second greatest command was to love your neighbor as yourself. He illustrated this with the story of the Good Samaritan who demonstrated kindness, which is basically love in action. The dictionary defines kindness as: "generous, hospitable, warmhearted and helpful, expressing concern or sympathy for others."

I know a mother who is very project minded. She has a driving, dominant personality. As a result, when she is in the midst of one of her projects at home she may focus almost exclusively on the project. At those times, the children and their tender feelings often get hurt. Fortunately, she recognized that these unintentional wounds still hurt her children, and so she made kindness a family project. She told her kids she needed to work on being kinder, and she also wanted them to be kinder to each other. She is now much more aware of how she treats the kids, and if their feelings get hurt they know to come to her privately and tell her in a respectful way.

This has resulted in the children being more open to her instructions on kindness. The family project has been a success for everyone involved.

A lot of women feel intimidated by the Proverbs 31 woman. She sold real estate, ran a household *and* a business, and was an excellent wife and mother. Throughout the chapter, her actions demonstrated her excellence. Only verse 26 describes how she speaks— when the Proverbs 31 woman speaks, moms should listen: "She opens her mouth in wisdom, the teaching of kindness is on her tongue." I'm sure her words of wisdom and kindness were aimed at her little ones. If teaching kindness was important enough to her in the midst of her busy life, it should be important to us in the midst of our busyness. The teaching of kindness should be part of every discussion after a conflict between the children. If they demonstrate kindness toward their siblings, then it will be much easier to treat their peers with kindness.

3. Integrity.

Integrity is like honesty. Honesty is truth in words, and integrity is honest words and actions integrated together. The dictionary defines integrity as "moral soundness." This is honesty that permeates a person if his words and actions are always consistent. The person who lacks honesty in words will lie, while the person who lacks honesty in actions will cheat or steal. The person of integrity stands in sharp contrast to those who believe that truth and moral values are not absolute but change according to the people or group.

Marie, mother of five, and grandmother of thirteen, said, "I am convinced that children are born liars. You don't have to teach them to lie." One story from my childhood that my kids especially like to hear is about the day I stole a girl's ring in Sunday School. I smuggled it home in my little patent leather purse. I lied in both my actions and my words. As the day progressed, the knot in my stomach grew bigger and bigger. I hid it in the bottom of a dresser drawer, but I was afraid to take it out for fear my sister would catch me. I was so miserable and afraid of being caught, that I eventually buried the ring in our backyard. After the story, we discuss how the ring lost its appeal because stealing and lying made me miserable.

In our home, any lie is treated seriously. After we take the child aside, he is punished, and we talk one on one. We talk about the importance of keeping a good reputation. Once a child lies, it becomes harder for me to believe them when they say they are telling the truth. I remind them that I always want to believe them, but if they lie, how will I be able to trust them. An honest reputation is a sad thing to lose. They must earn a reputation of honesty. If a child can get away with lying to a parent, then they will probably try lying to teachers and others.

A phrase my children often repeated was, "Mommy, I'm going to obey you, I'm going to obey you." I grew tired of hearing it repeated without seeing any actions to confirm it. One day this went on and on. Finally I told my children to show me by their actions that they would obey me. "Mommy, I'm showing by my actions," has now become a familiar phrase in our home.

4. Responsibility.

The dictionary defines responsible as, "able to be trusted or depended upon, reliable." If the parent is dependable or trustworthy this will encourage the same traits in the child. But if the parent fails to keep promises to the child, it will be hard to teach the child to be responsible.

The child who is reliable or dependable can be trusted even when no one is watching. The ultimate test for responsibility is the child's behavior when a babysitter comes. Does the child still follow the family rules, or does he try to convince the babysitter that all sorts of wrong activity is allowed. If your child passes the babysitter test with flying colors, you're on your way to having a responsible child.

A mother I know has a diabetic daughter. The mother cannot be with her all day at school to monitor her sugar intake. If a classmate brings cupcakes to celebrate his birthday, the mother can't be there to make sure the daughter doesn't eat one. The girl knows she must accept full responsibility for what she eats. She has become very responsible. As time goes on, this ability to control herself will extend into other areas of her life.

Many children today don't know how to take responsibility for their own actions. The more children are shielded from the consequences of their own wrong actions, the more irresponsible they will become. A parent who shields her children from experiencing the consequences of their own actions is undermining the natural law of cause and effect. The children who have been shielded from their own consequences will one day commit a major offense and the parent will be powerless to shield them any longer. It's far more merciful and wise to teach them responsibility with little episodes when the stakes are low.

When my second son was one-year-old, he would wake up from a nap and begin bailing out all his stuffed animals from the crib. This harmless action kept him amused while he waited to be released. I could have easily picked up all the animals and put them in the crib, but I saw this was an opportunity to begin teaching responsibility. I held him in my arms and flew him down to the floor so he could pick up an animal. Then I lifted him to the crib so he could drop it in. This continued until all the animals were safely in the crib. Then I told him he was a BIG boy because he picked up all his animals. He beamed with pride.

This was the start of the rule in our home. If you make a mess, you get to clean it up—some messes, of course, require Mom's assistance. This rule forces the kids to stop and think of the mess they'll have to clean up before they make it.

When a child disobeys and gets punished, he may get angry. If he does, I always ask him, "Who broke the rule?" To which he invariably replies, "I did." Then I remind him that he chose to suffer the punishment by breaking the rule.

5. Discernment.

In order to understand discernment, we must look first at two terms: *knowledge* and *wisdom*. *Knowledge* is accumulating facts or information. *Wisdom* is knowing how to apply the knowledge. The dictionary defines discernment as: "to perceive differences, to make distinctions." When a child is exposed to ideas or people, he needs to draw a line between God's truth and the world's error. A lot of ideas are a blend of truth and error. The child needs discernment as he sorts out what to believe, and what to reject.

181

In 1 Kings 3, young King Solomon was given the wish of a lifetime. God appeared to him in a dream and said He would give Solomon anything he wanted. He asked God for an understanding heart so he could discern between good and evil. God was so pleased with Solomon's request, that He gave Solomon riches, fame, and peace in addition to making him the wisest man in the world. The child who has an understanding heart and can discern between good and evil will be spared much grief as he grows up.

In our society there are so many ideas and philosophies that sound good on the surface, but under careful scrutiny are based on faulty and often immoral logic. I want my children to discern God's truth from the world's error. This error may be in a television show, a song on the radio, a book, or a video. It may even come from a friend.

When a person is trained to detect counterfeit bills, all his time is spent with real dollars, carefully examining and feeling thousands and thousands of real dollars. He knows the real thing so well, that the first time a counterfeit is slipped in the pile, he can see and feel it instantly. In the same way, I feed my children a steady diet of Bible stories and classics that have a solid moral base. These stories can be found not only in books but also in videos, so their television time is also constructive. In addition, I talk with them about wise and foolish characters and the consequences that came as the result of their actions. Not only do I want my children to be discerning about ideas, but they should also be discerning about people. Psalm 1:1-2 says, "Blessed is the man who does not walk in the counsel of the wicked or stand in the way of sinners or sit in the seat of mockers. But his delight is in the law of the LORD, and on his law he meditates day and night."

I also pray for my children to be careful in their choice of friends, so both they and their friends will encourage each other to do right. Many times I have told my children to choose friends not only by their words, but also by their actions. They need to make sure that both align. When they don't align, the children should be suspicious.

One day out of the blue, my son said, "Mom, before I get married, I'm going to watch my future wife real carefully. She'll be nice to me, but I want to see how she treats other people. Then I'll find out what she's really like." At the tender age of six, he was already internalizing discernment. He has learned to watch people's actions, especially when they don't think they're being observed.

6. Confidence.

The dictionary defines confidence as, "having assurance or certainty of success." This is a quiet assurance or sense of security. This is vastly different from pride, which is defined as, "an excessively high opinion of oneself." A child's confidence should be based on Jesus. He needs to know that throughout the day, no matter what comes his way, Jesus will be with him. In fact, when facing insurmountable odds or fierce opposition, the child must know that he and Jesus are a majority.

The stories of David and Goliath, and Daniel in the lion's den, can be told countless times. Parents can end the story by asking, "How could little David kill big Goliath?" or "How did Daniel survive the lions?" The answer to both is, "God saved them because He is the strongest one of all." If God can help David, then God can help *all* children with the giants in their young lives.

Whenever a child faces a fearful situation, have him pray and ask God for help. Proverbs 3:24 is an excellent verse for young children to memorize if they're afraid of the dark. "When you lie down, you will not be afraid; when you lie down your sleep will be sweet." If a child awakens in the middle of the night from a bad dream, I have him sing, "Yes, Jesus loves me. He will protect me. Yes, Jesus loves me. The Bible tells me so." If a child is afraid of a bully at school, have him learn Proverbs 1:33—"But whoever listens to me will live in safety and be at ease, without fear of harm." Remind a child that if he stands up and faces his fear, it will grow smaller and smaller each time.

This can also apply to feeling confident about doing well at school. Each morning before our children leave the van we stop and pray, asking God to give each child a perfect day at school. With each successful day that passes, their confidence in God and themselves grows.

7. Contentment.

The dictionary defines contentment as, "not desiring more than one has, satisfied."

King Solomon was the wisest, wealthiest and most powerful king in ancient times. Yet with all this he wasn't happy. He looked at his life and despised it saying, "Vanity of vanities, all is vanity." Ecclesiastes 12:8. The problem he suffered from was a lack of contentment. He had an insatiable desire for more, always more. When he was older, he looked back on his youth and regretted it was gone. His aging body was slowing down and he knew death would claim him one day. He serves as a sad example of someone who started out with noble aspirations but became disillusioned along the way. Possessing discernment did not give him contentment with all that he had.

The Apostle Paul stood in stark contrast to King Solomon. He was a brilliant man of high Jewish standing, yet he could say from prison, "For I have learned to be content whatever the circumstances. I know what it is to be in need, and I know what it is to have plenty. I have learned the secret of being content in any and every situation, whether well fed or hungry, whether living in plenty or in want" (Philippians 4:11-12).

Discontented people are all around us. They are from every socioeconomic group. They are driven by the insatiable craving for more, a bigger house, a better car, another promotion. But once they have these things they decide that the house still isn't big enough, the car isn't good enough, and the promotion wasn't high enough. The sad thing is that these people will never have enough. As a result they can't enjoy what they have. This attitude of discontent can be started innocently in childhood by indulgent parents who want to satisfy all their children's needs as a demonstration of their love.

In our school, the day after Christmas vacation was always fun as the students came back with new Christmas gifts like coats, clothes, books, or art supplies. One student, Mary Anne, came to my desk to show me her Christmas outfit. She twirled around and said, "What do you think, Miss Johnson? It's all designer labels!" Her blouse, vest, skirt, and patent leather shoes made a very classy outfit. Then she added, "My mom told me that this outfit costs more than any of her outfits." This girl was eight years old, with an outfit more expensive than her mother's. What will they give her next year when she's nine? Then what would she get when she was ten? The parents were setting themselves up in the trap of always needing to buy bigger and better gifts.

Naturally parents love their children and want to give them good gifts. But we need to give them gifts that will help them to be truly happy and content. Creating in them the desire for bigger and better will rob them of contentment with all they possess.

In contrast, if children are to learn contentment, they must learn to enjoy playing with the toys they already have. When they ask for a bigger or better toy like a friend owns, they should be reminded about the great toys they already own. We try to downplay any comparisons. The children get new clothes when they need them, and new toys are given for birthdays and Christmas. Each child receives three or four gifts from us. We give our children games and books along with toys. These help us spend fun time together. I also encourage my children to have adventures together. They learn to make fun together wherever they go. They don't need a ton of toys, and are developing the priceless trait of contentment.

Many people devote their entire lives to the pursuit of happiness only to have it elude them. Here's a recipe for happiness from Mary Engelbreit, that has captured the missing ingredient: "Combine 4 parts *Contentment*, 2 parts *Joy*, and 1 part *Pleasure*. These ingredients must be grown in one's own garden. Sometimes they need to be obtained from a good friend. When so procured, a fair return must be made else *Happiness* spoils and becomes *Trouble*. Sometimes *Discontent* and *Ambition* have been combined in a desire to obtain *Happiness*, but *Fame* or *Wealth* have resulted—and those who have tasted these say they are inferior substitutes."

8. Patience.

The dictionary defines patience as "calm endurance, tolerant understanding." Thousands of coffee mugs across America state, "Lord, give me patience, and I need it NOW!" It's a challenge to be still and wait for the slow driver blocking the turn lane. It's hard to be calm when the checkout line is long, the children are complaining, and the ice cream in the shopping cart is melting.

When I'm impatient, I can only see my inconvenience. This reveals my selfishness as I fail to see the needs of others. Often when I'm three minutes late—and trying to recover time on the road—I get impatient with the slow driver who's blocking my lane. It doesn't occur to me to be sensitive to the slow driver, and that maybe he's lost and needs help. All I care about is getting me to my destination. The more sensitive I am of others, the more patient I'll become.

That horrible hour before dinner when my children hit meltdown is a great time to start teaching patience. As they grumble and complain about hunger and almost anything else, I remind them that every time I have to stop and talk to them, dinner is being delayed. If they want dinner faster, they can help me and we will eat sooner. Often they will set the table, put food out, or entertain the baby so I'm free to cook. My toddler knows if he quietly sits in his chair and waits, I'll give him a cracker and some juice. Then I'll thank him for being so patient. This allows me to buzz around the kitchen and not worry about stepping on him. He knows dinner will come faster as a result.

Later when we're sitting around the table, I'm usually busy dishing up the children's food and cutting it. If one of them starts chanting, "More juice, more juice, MORE JUICE!" I ask him if my hands are busy. Then I tell him whenever he sees my hands are busy, he must be patient and wait quietly. When my hands are empty, he can ask and I'll gladly help him. Much of patience is being aware of the other person and thinking less of self.

There are also those days when I'm desperately trying to get out the door on time. My arms are loaded with purse, diaper bag, books and anything else I need to take. Two small people are clinging to my legs fussing and whining. In the midst of all this noise and confusion, I try to think of anything else I may have forgotten to bring as the walls seem to crash in around me. My natural response is to explode. But if I just stop long enough to pray an SOS prayer, "Dear Jesus, please help me!" He'll get me through as a cool, calm mom—able to leap tall buildings or handle two little children.

We live in an *instant* society. If we want dinner, we just stick food in the microwave. *Zap!* Out comes dinner. We have instant credit, ATMs, video stores, and pizza delivery to give us *what we want when we want it*. In such a society, our children will grow to expect everything *instantly* unless we work to instill some patience in them.

9. Perseverance.

The dictionary defines perseverance as, "steadfastness, endurance, in pursuit of a desired end."

Life is full of problems. The difference between those who succeed and those who fail is often one of perseverance. Most successful people have looked failure in the face and determined to learn from their failures and move on. That's what I want for my children. But if I'm constantly following them around and intervening every time I see them about to fail, I'll prevent them from developing this important trait.

Thomas Edison failed hundreds of times in his attempts to invent a light bulb. If he had quit trying, he would have faded into obscurity, and the world would have waited in darkness until someone else brought them light. But Edison persevered in the face of repeated failures that would have daunted a lesser man.

Sir Edmund Hillary, the first man to climb Mount Everest, failed to reach the top many times. He lost a man in his last failed attempt. Undaunted by this loss, he looked at a mural of Mount Everest on the wall and said, "Mount Everest, you defeated me. But I will return. And I will defeat you. Because you can't get any bigger and I can." In 1959, with a Sherpa guide, Tenzing Norgay, Hillary climbed successfully to the summit of Mount Everest.

If children are to succeed in life, they must surmount obstacles. We love our children and want to protect them from difficulty and pain. Yet if we overprotect them, they will never learn to face little obstacles in their little world. If they learn to face little obstacles, they will gain confidence to face bigger obstacles later in life.

When a child is first learning to walk, falling down is part of the learning process. I would never allow my children to walk into anything that might be dangerous, but I wanted them to have the experience of falling down, getting up, and brushing themselves off. When one of them did, I would say, "Oh look at you, you got up all by yourself. What a BIG person you are!" As a result, my children have learned that it's okay to fall, all they have to do is get up and life moves on. This is the start of planting the seed of perseverance in their little lives.

Life's pressures are opportunities for growth. James 1:2-4 says: "Consider it pure joy, my brothers, whenever you face trials of many kinds, because you know that the testing of your faith develops perseverance. Perseverance must finish its work so that you may be mature and complete, not lacking anything."

As a child's world gets larger and he spends more time at school and with friends, the chances of him encountering storms will increase. Maybe there's a bully on the playground he must deal with. Now the parent needs to encourage the child as he faces his own storm, and understand that this is just as big, if not bigger, to him as any storm the parent may face. The child must see it as an opportunity for growth as he depends on God to help him. So, how does a parent help? First the father or mother must be available to listen and sympathize, "If a bully said that to me, I would be sad too." Then the parent needs to provide good counsel on ways to avoid the bully, teaching the child to rely on God. The parent should only intervene when necessary. As a parent helps the child to endure storms, the child will become stronger.

As our children grow, we should look for opportunities to encourage them to develop this trait when they face life's problems. Once children are in school they need to remember to complete their homework, deal with other children bothering them, and cooperate with the teacher. If a parent always comes to rescue their children from their problems, the children will never develop this priceless trait. Wise parents will sympathize with their children and give them the tools they need to face their problems. Parents should try to intervene less and less as a child grows, but should always be available to encourage and give wise counsel.

A friend, Martha, has a nine-year-old son who enjoys looking at all the electronic gadgets at Radio Shack. One day he saw the ultimate gadget, and decided he needed to have it. The price was $40. The family wasn't economically deprived, and it would have been easy for Martha to write out a check for $40. Instead, she decided her son could work for it by doing chores around the house. Because he had a goal that he was working toward, he was motivated and worked hard. Once the money was saved, he went down and proudly bought his gadget, which means more to him now because it represents a month's worth of labor to him. Martha is glad she helped him learn this valuable lesson.

Many children today don't have to work for anything, they just get whatever they want, and they will expect everything to continue to come easy to them later in life. Because they do, they will more often fail at difficult projects. But a child who has worked toward some goals and obtained them, will become an adult who will succeed with long term goals.

A Final Note

King Solomon has been used as a positive example, and as a negative example. In the same way, if any of your children have only a few of the nine character traits, but are lacking the others, this imbalance could cause them grief. Seek to instill balanced character in your children.

Your children want to be just like you. Boys want to be like their dads and girls like their mothers. Make the most of this natural tendency, and help them be all they should be. Adolescence comes all too quickly, so while your children are young, lay a foundation of solid moral character that will help them travel victoriously through the battle of adolescence.

They say that a tree is best measured when it is down on the ground. In the days that followed the assassination of Abraham Lincoln, world famous men wrote about Lincoln and his place in history. Walt Whitman, the American writer, said, "Lincoln was the greatest figure on the crowded canvas of the nineteenth century." Henrik Ibsen, the Norwegian playwright, wrote that Lincoln was "the foremost son of democracy in the Western World." Leo Tolstoy, the Russian novelist wrote, "Lincoln was a world folk legend. He had peculiar moral powers and greatness of character. He was what Beethoven is in music, Dante in poetry, and Raphael in painting. If he had failed to be president, he would be no doubt just as great, but only God could appreciate it. Lincoln was the real giant of all the world's national heroes. We are still too near his greatness and so can hardly appreciate his divine power, but after a few centuries more, later generations will find him considerably bigger than we do."

Truly Abraham Lincoln was a great man. What caused his great moral character to grow into a massive tree? He gave the credit to his stepmother, Sarah Bush

Lincoln. He called her, "My angel mother." He said, "She has been my best friend in this world." She exerted a "more profound influence on his developing mind and character than any other single person." At the age of nine, his mother died. As a result, he sank into gloomy spells at times. When he was ten, his father married Sarah. She was a warm, kind woman of dignity. She was sensitive to his melancholy moods, and loved him like her own. Later she referred to him as her "best child."

A stepmother made a profound impact on world history. Nearly 180 years ago when Sarah Bush Lincoln was planting character seeds in a little boy's life, she never dreamed they would grow into greatness.

Now, it's our turn to plant the right character seeds in the little lives God has placed in our care.

15
Three Final Subjects

Before leaving this crucial topic of child discipline, three final subjects must be addressed: *prayer, mentor, and guilt.*

Prayer

Prayer has been mentioned throughout this book. Its importance can never be underestimated.

As a teacher, I prayed for my students in the summer before I even knew their names. One day a week I devoted my prayer time to the children God would place in my care.

Once school started, those prayer times took on more significance as I prayed through my entire class list. While I prayed for each child, I asked God to help in any trouble area, whether it was academic, emotional, social, or spiritual. I also asked God to help me with my attitude toward a student if I struggled with being fair to him. Some mornings before school started, I might sit in a struggling student's desk and pray for God's help as I sought to reach him. Often I saw change in a child, as he finally "got it." More important, I felt change in me as my wrong attitude melted.

Now as a mother, I'm committed to praying for my children. Even before they were born, I prayed for God's blessing and protection on them. Now I pray for them daily. Often I pray for their current dilemmas and discipline problems. I also pray for their friends, for them to have the courage to withstand the temptations of adolescence, and for their future marriage partners. Many times I've seen God at work in my children's daily lives as He faithfully helps them. He also gives me wisdom and a right attitude. Some days in the heat of escalating emotions, I remember to stop and seek help. When I do, He helps me to diffuse volatile situations.

Mentor

Whether you are a parent or a teacher, it's wise for you to find a mentor. Look around at other parents or teachers who are more experienced than you. Find someone you respect, whose children or students are turning out well-balanced. Watch them and notice what they're doing. If you feel comfortable, ask them how they deal with specific discipline problems. They won't mind—they'll feel honored that you asked, and will gladly give you an answer. A mentor has been where you now are. She has gained valuable insights that are priceless.

As a single woman, I frequently watched young mothers interact with their children. I hoped that one day I would also be a mother. I formed many ideas about good mothering just from watching. Now that I am a mother, I've found a mentor whose children are grown. She gives me wisdom and encouragement.

Mentors remind us that life is a constant state of growing and learning. This is especially true for parents who just figure out the best way to deal with their two-year-old and then realize their child has changed. Now at nearly three, the child encounters new problems. Since the mentor has already been there, she can give you the larger perspective.

Guilt

Both parents and teachers have a great responsibility as they seek to train the next generation. As a result, it's very easy to see their faults and feel guilty.

On the last day of school I always had my students fill out an anonymous evaluation of their year in my class. Each child listed the three things they liked the most about third grade, and then listed the three things they liked least. I told them to be honest since they didn't write their names, and I had already completed their report cards. This was their chance to help me be a better teacher. After I collected all the evaluations, I hugged each one and wished them a wonderful summer. Once my room was empty, I would sit down and started reading the evaluations. Most of them listed favorite and least favorite subjects.

One time, however, one evaluation form jumped off the stack at me. I instantly recognized the handwriting. It told me that I had accused her of lying even though she hadn't lied. She went on to say that she tried to defend herself, but I wouldn't believe her.

I must have read that note at least three times. I vaguely remembered an incident that happened months earlier. Even though I couldn't remember all of the details, it was clearly branded on her memory. As a lump grew in my throat, I longed to have this girl back in my class so I could apologize to her and give her a BIG hug. I struggled deciding what to do next. Should I call her home and ask her forgiveness, or would she be embarrassed that her note was no longer anonymous? I eventually dropped it, because I didn't want her to think I had violated her privacy by "figuring out" it came from her. Then I prayed and asked God to forgive my insensitivity. I asked Him to help me be more sensitive with my new students in the fall.

If it were to happen again today, however, I know without a doubt that I would call and ask her forgiveness. I still feel regret that I let her walk out of my life with the issue unresolved.

I have yet to meet a mother who doesn't feel guilt about her own inadequacies as a mother. Motherhood is the guiltiest profession of all. A mother loves her children deeply and desires to do what is best for them. But a mother can never be perfect, and so she will often feel guilty for having failed at something. There are two main sources of this guilt: *unrealistic expectations* and *losing our tempers*.

When my first child was born, I gladly poured my best into him. Then our second child came and I struggled to give our first child as much individual time as I did before the birth of our second. At the same time, I knew I wasn't giving my new baby as much individual time as I gave my first baby when he was a newborn.

Thus the juggling act began. Soon I was pregnant again with my third, then my fourth. As each new child entered our home I was elated. Yet this was always tempered with the reality that each child would not be able to receive as much individual attention as an only child receives. Instead I needed to juggle faster and faster so no one would be dropped.

Even though I do the best I can, I still struggle with false guilt because I'm not able to give more of myself. I'm so glad that God is gracious and doesn't demand such perfection from me. He knows I have a finite number of hours in each day. He knows I also need to be a loving wife, cook, laundress, chauffeur, nurse, accountant, gardener, and maid—to mention a few.

Twenty-four hours a day including holidays and weekends a mother is on the job. Thus our children have the opportunity to see us at our worst when we're sick, impatient, or exhausted.

A friend, Melba, received a phone call from her adult daughter. "Oh Mom, I really blew it today! I lost my cool. The kids were fighting. It was one thing after the other. I think I yelled at them all day long. Now they're fast asleep, and I feel so bad. I wonder if I've scarred them for life. Mother, you never yelled at us. I just grew up feeling loved. How did you do it?"

There was silence on the other end of the line as Melba remembered those days long ago. Those days when four small children whined and quarreled, pushing against the limits, pushing against her composure. Days when she blew it and yelled angrily at her children, and nights when she felt guilty about the verbal anger she had hurled at them. She often wondered, too, if she had scarred them. In calm moments she would go to them and seek their forgiveness.

Now 25 years later, God had graciously wiped from her daughter's memory those days of frustration and anger. Melba softly replied, "Oh, I had my days when I lost my temper. But God was good and caused all of the wonderful days to stay in your mind, while the few angry days have faded away. As long as you have an overriding atmosphere of love and warmth in your home, the children will remember that. As you ask them to forgive you, God will graciously wash away those few times when you yelled."

References

Dobson, James. *The New Dare to Discipline.* Tyndale House Publishers, 1992.

Engelbreit, Mary. *Recipe for Happiness.* Antioch Publishing Co., 1992.

Hendricks, Howard. *Communicating Values to Your Children.* Moody Contemporary Issues Series.

Hickok, Lorena A. *The Touch of Magic. The Story of Helen Keller's Great Teacher: Anne Sullivan.* Dodd, Mead and Co., 1961

Sandburg, Carl. *ABRAHAM LINCOLN The Prairie Years and the War Years.* The Reader's Digest Association, 1970.

Turecki, Stanley, and Leslie Tonner. *The Difficult Child.* Bantam Books, 1989.

Wender, Paul H. M. D. *The Hyperactive Child, Adolescent and Adult.* Oxford Press, 1987.

U.S. Bureau of the Census. Statistical Abstract of the United States. 1993, 113th Edition.